β

CW00541688

Jodi Bilske

Born and raised in the Northern Territory, **Toni Tapp Coutts** has had a varied career, from living on cattle stations, riding in campdrafts and barrel racing, to owning a variety store in outback Borroloola and a dress boutique in Katherine.

She was shortlisted in the 2002 NT Literary Awards for her story 'Daisy & Dora'. In 2009 she spent time at Varuna, The National Writers' House in Katoomba, NSW, to work on *A Sunburnt Childhood*. An earlier version of chapter 7 entitled 'Walking the Wet' was published in *Meanjin Quarterly* in March 2010.

Toni is a leader in her community in Katherine, working for the Victoria Daly Regional Council and organising leadership groups for women within the vast council area. She has been an elected member of the Katherine Town Council for more than ten years. A mother of three, she lives in Katherine with her husband, Shaun. She is the aunt of *MasterChef* 2013 runner-up Lynton Tapp and of *The Voice* 2014 finalist Holly Tapp.

A Sunburnt CHILDHOOD

Growing up in the Territory

TONI TAPP COUTTS

hachette
AUSTRALIA

People of Aboriginal or Torres Strait Islander heritage are advised that this book contains names and photographs of people who are deceased or may be deceased.

Unless otherwise credited, photos are from Toni Tapp Coutts's personal collection.

hachette
AUSTRALIA

First published in Australia and New Zealand in 2016
by Hachette Australia
(an imprint of Hachette Australia Pty Limited)
Level 17, 207 Kent Street, Sydney NSW 2000
www.hachette.com.au

This edition published in 2017

10 9 8 7 6 5 4 3 2 1

National Library of Australia
Cataloguing-in-Publication data

Tapp Coutts, Toni, 1955 – author.
A sunburnt childhood/Toni Tapp Coutts.

978 0 7336 3781 0 (paperback)

Tapp Coutts, Toni, 1955 – Childhood and youth.
Cattle properties – Northern Territory.
Country life – Northern Territory – Biography.
Women – Northern Territory – Biography.
Killarney Station (N.T.)

636.213092

Cover design by Luke Causby/Blue Cork
Cover photographs courtesy of Getty Images (silhouette of stockman and cattle)
   and Toni Tapp Coutts
Text design by Bookhouse, Sydney
Typeset in 12/19 pt Sabon LT Pro by Bookhouse, Sydney
Printed and bound in Australia by Griffin Press, Adelaide, an Accredited ISO AS/NZS 14001:2009
Environmental Management System printer

MIX
Paper from
responsible sources
FSC® C009448
www.fsc.org

The paper this book is printed on is certified against the Forest Stewardship Council® Standards. Griffin Press holds FSC chain of custody certification SGS-COC-005088. FSC promotes environmentally responsible, socially beneficial and economically viable management of the world's forests.

*To the people of Killarney 1960–1993, to my parents
Bill and June Tapp, to my nine siblings and all those who
stood by us through the best and the worst of times.*

CONTENTS

PROLOGUE

THE LAND WHERE I GREW UP IS VAST AND FLAT. WHEN I first came to Killarney Station, there was barely a tree to be seen, and that sparse vista stretched all the way to the horizon, 2819 square kilometres, larger than the European country of Luxembourg, about as untamed as you'd imagine. Wherever I looked, there was Killarney with its feral cattle, its even wilder stockmen and the promise of a new life for my mother, my brother and sister, and me.

In the dry season Killarney was brown and grey and khaki, with only the red dirt to provide some relief. In the wet season the creek would swell, the trees turned bright green, the grass grew emerald and the dirt became vermilion. It was so beautiful, and the land would heave with so much life, that we could almost forget that the dry season would come. But, inevitably, the ground would crack and the creek would become a trickle, and the cycle would continue again.

On Killarney there was no getting away from the realities of the climate. That cycle of life in the Northern Territory dictated everything: how we lived, how we worked. We couldn't hide inside a comfortable home – we didn't have one. We couldn't run away to a nearby town – Katherine was the closest and it was over 250 kilometres away.

When we moved to Killarney, I was five years old and my mother had fallen in love with a man called Bill Tapp. It was Bill Tapp who brought us to Killarney: his home, his kingdom, his crazy dream come true. It was Bill Tapp who changed all of our lives.

Killarney was ruled by Bill Tapp. My mother, June, reigned at his side. The pair of them had personalities bigger than the land they surveyed, and they ran our family with love and strength. Bill Tapp was the caretaker of not just his own family but of the people who worked for him. There were lonely men who were running away from their pasts; young families Bill Tapp would take under his wing; and a camp of Aboriginal workers and their families, who were an integral part of our life.

From very early on, he was always called 'Bill Tapp'. There were so many Bills working at Killarney: there was Bill Hart, the cook, and Bill Ardill, the bore man; my mother's uncle, Bill Forscutt, who was a general handyman; and Mum's brother, another Bill Forscutt, who was called 'Boof'. Everyone called Bill Tapp 'Bill Tapp': the workers, the kids, Mum, Nana, the bank manager, and the women on the radio telephone exchange. None of the children ever called him 'Dad' – in later years I would sometimes tease him and call him 'Dad', but he would grow uncomfortable and gruffly say, 'BILL TAPP,' in response.

My childhood was spent taking care of my brothers and sisters, playing with my friends and falling in love with the land I grew up on. I was happy on Killarney. I couldn't imagine a better place to live, or a better life to lead, even if to most people's way of thinking it would have seemed as though we had nothing. That 'nothing' was rich with love and adventure. It was everything.

While Bill Tapp took care of running the land and the business, my mother ran the household and the camp. They were a formidable pair – until it all fell apart. But that was a long way past my childhood and a long time in the making.

We'll get to that. First, I have to be born.

Chapter 1

IN THE BEGINNING

IN ALICE SPRINGS, ON A SCORCHING HOT MORNING IN November 1955, as the star-studded horizon dulled and the Southern Cross slipped off the side of the earth followed by the Scorpion, I made my entry into the world. I was the first-born grandchild on both sides of the family.

Alice Springs was a dusty desert town; it still is. The hot, harsh climate has a roller-coaster of temperatures ranging from an Antarctic minus to a murderous 45 degrees Celsius. The red desert is as flat as a breadboard, with staggered ranges popping up at intervals to create ancient gorges that whisper the stories of the Arrernte people who have walked the land for the last 40 000 years. The sky is a million light years away and yet, at night, feels so close you could just stretch your hand and touch the Milky Way above your head. My sign of Scorpio hangs just east of the Southern Cross, its tail curled low across the dark night, claws reaching out into the black universe.

The Aboriginal name for Alice Springs is Mparntwe. In 1955, the Aboriginal people lived on the banks of the Todd River at the fringes of town in skimpy humpies made from paperbark trees and scraps of rusty corrugated iron. They were forbidden to cohabit with white people.

At the time of my birth, Alice Springs had been gripped by a devastating drought for ten years and red sand hills were piled around the town, right up to our front door, covering suburban fences, roads and footpaths, old cars, gardens and anything that had not been moved in the past year. Alice was a tough place for anyone to live in. It was the year before the Melbourne Olympics and the rest of Australia was leaping into the world of modernisation. With a population of just 1500, Alice Springs was still an outback town without television or telephones, where fridges were kerosene and few families had washing machines or a family car. Most women stayed at home to raise their children.

My mother – June Forscutt as she was born and June Clements as she was then – was no different. My parents were typical of the 1950s: childhood sweethearts who grew up in a small town, got pregnant, got married and had children. My father, Terry Clements, drank, worked and socialised with his friends too much. He worked at the Welfare Department earning twenty pounds a week, of which he gave my mother seven pounds to run the house and clothe and feed the family. The rest of his income was spent on his hobbies and social life: racehorses, playing cricket, football and drinking with his mates at the club, a common and convenient lifestyle for the men of Alice Springs, and too bad for the women if they didn't like it.

On the day my mother went into labour, my father was playing cricket; after receiving the news, he continued to play. My mother was unimpressed but that was just the way things were: Dad would get on with whatever he was doing while Mum got on with the business of whatever she was doing – in this case, giving birth.

Mum tells me that she remembers the day I was born as the day she started reading *Gone with the Wind* and fell in love with Rhett Butler. My mum didn't make a fuss about giving birth in a stark delivery room with nurses in starched white uniforms and caps like the Flying Nun wore. Instead, she made herself at home in the maternity ward right away. Maybe she had a sense that it was a place she would visit many times. Mum told me that the cranky old matron slapped her hands as she gripped the cast-iron bedhead in the final throes of giving birth. My arrival was swift and easy; I was born in the early hours of the morning and promptly taken to the nursery. Mum was wheeled out onto the verandah and left to rest under a big, slow-moving fan.

A few hours later the old matron came out and huffed, 'Well, Mrs Clements, would you like to see your baby today?'

My mother looked up in surprise. She had become so immersed in reading *Gone with the Wind* that she had forgotten she'd had a baby. She took me from Matron's arms, attached me to her breast and continued reading her book. As I was to learn, this was typical of my mother's ability to be waylaid by her fascination with the world beyond her immediate experience.

I was called Toni because Mum was in love with the Hollywood actor Anthony Quinn. On her first day out shopping after my birth, she left me asleep in the pram at the butcher shop while she caught a taxi home. She arrived home with the groceries and no baby, so she had to return to town in the taxi to pick me up – finding me fast asleep in the corner.

—

My mother, June Caroline Forscutt, was born in Cobar, New South Wales on 12 December 1935 and grew up in the small town of Weethalle, about halfway between Cobar and Canberra. She was the second child in what would become a family of five brothers and two sisters. Her mother was one of ten children, a fun-loving woman with a great sense of humour who loved to dance and sing, while her father loved to sing and talk politics. He had a small garage in town where he fixed farm machinery. Next to the garage was the family's house, with holes in the walls and a flapping tin roof and one dull light globe in the lounge. The Forscutts slept three to a bed, with thin grey army blankets and handmade pillowcase-style covers filled with old jumpers. The jumpers fell in lumps and bumps to the sides of the cover and created little warmth. The children rode three astride a horse to school and did not have any shoes. They were given a lunch of a slice of bread smeared with a thin layer of fat, more commonly known as dripping.

Both June's parents had brothers serving in Darwin during the Second World War. When the soldiers returned to Weethalle they told stories about the last frontier and the lure of work, gold mines and crocodile hunting. This was enough for my grandfather Nick Forscutt to decide, in 1947, to pack up his wife, Gladys, and their six children (as they were then) to leave the almost destitute life they had in New South Wales and head north.

My grandfather went first, leaving Weethalle with his brother-in-law Frankie Hennings, who had been in Darwin during the war, to travel to Hayes Creek, a small gold-mining town 150 kilometres south-east of Darwin. They had to find somewhere to live before sending for Nana and the rest of the kids. Three months later, a family friend named David Fairlie drove my grandmother and the children, all under the age of fourteen, to Hayes Creek in a Model T Ford with two double mattresses strapped to the roof. They took a dog with them, specifically for throwing into the rivers – they had been told about the big crocodiles in the Territory and that the only way to tell if there was a croc near a crossing was to throw a dog in. If the dog survived it was safe to cross the river, and if a crocodile took the dog it was still safe to cross, as the croc would have had a feed and therefore would not eat the humans.

My mum was eleven. Nana was nursing her six-month-old daughter, Lynette, as she travelled the thousands of kilometres through outback Queensland, across the Barkly Tableland, on to the Stuart Highway and north through Mataranka and Katherine to Hayes Creek before they settled at Adelaide River, which had been an army base and hospital during the war, when Darwin was the home of Australia's major military base. (The Adelaide River War Cemetery was the final resting place for many killed during the bombing of Darwin.) Mum says that on the trip up they had a tent to camp in, but that they only slept in it once because a bull got into it and ripped it to pieces.

The family lived in a large open tin shed. There was no school in Adelaide River, so the kids spent most of their time exploring the river and watching the trains and army trucks come and go – even though the war was over, the army was still at the hub of life in the town.

Just two months after arriving in the Top End, baby Lynette developed a high fever. Mum remembers Lynette having convulsions and Nana putting her into a metal tub and mixing mustard powder into the water in an attempt to bring her temperature down.

Lynette died not long afterwards of a brain aneurysm. It happened that the doctor from Darwin who visited Katherine once a month was returning to Darwin through Hayes Creek at the time the baby died. My nana nursed her dead daughter on the arduous and rough trip along the Stuart Highway – not so much a highway as a dirt road – to bury her baby in a cemetery in Darwin. One can only imagine the deep sadness Gladys must have felt, to be in a hot, strange place where she knew no one, having left her mother and sisters way down in the cold south. My mother remembers the day clearly, the devastation she felt for her mother and the loss of her baby sister. She remembers her anger when, a day later, her father and his friends set up to play their nightly card games at the dining table while Nana stood in the dark, looking out into the desolate night. The death was not discussed again; it was like Lynette just disappeared out of their lives overnight.

Baby Lynette Forscutt was buried in the Old Darwin Cemetery under the name of Baby Fawcett, the surname of another family living at Adelaide River at the same time. A mistake was made during the registration of Lynette's death and it can't be corrected, so Baby Fawcett she remains.

———

While my grandfather was keen on the idea of setting up his own gold mine and going crocodile hunting, the reality of having to support and educate his young family weighed heavily on his mind so they packed up and left Adelaide River, moving down the track to Katherine, where he took up a job at the Katherine Power House. Katherine stands at the junction of two major roads: the Stuart Highway and the Victoria Highway. When my grandparents moved there it had about four streets and not many more people. Today it's a thriving town of over 10 000 inhabitants; it services an area of around 350 000 square kilometres, comprising remote Aboriginal communities, massive pastoral properties, mines and roadhouses and including Tindal air force base, home of the FA18s and 75 Squadron.

The family lived on the banks of the Katherine River, above the hot springs, in a shed similar in style to the Sydney Williams huts built by the army, which look just like a corrugated-iron version of a child's drawing of a house – a square with a door in the middle, rough-cut windows either side and a sloping roof. They soon settled into outback life and their house was always full of people. The children walked, often barefoot, through the long grass to the one-teacher school, and the family's social lives revolved around fundraising for the Country Women's Association (CWA), playing tennis and picnicking on the banks of the Katherine River. My grandparents had their seventh and final child, Sue, in 1948.

My mother's family was loud, boisterous and outgoing, and everyone had to look after themselves. The wood-fired stove burned twenty-four hours a day, with a large steel kettle boiling water for cooking and the endless pot of tea, and for warm baths in cold weather. After school, the kids played in the river that ran just below the back door – during the dry season the Katherine River runs through the town at a low enough level to be fairly safe. My mother was popular with all the boys and not so popular with the girls. She was smart, competitive and always wanted to win. She shared her high school holidays with many of the Stolen Generation 'half-castes', who had been taken from their Aboriginal families. They played football, tennis and cricket and spent all their spare time swimming at the Low Level, so named as there was a low car bridge and a weir, a spot where the paperbark trees towered and the river ran shallow in the dry season. It was a raging red torrent in the wet season.

The Forscutt family were close and Gladys adored her husband, Nick, who was a staunch Labor man. My grandmother had no interest in politics but she supported her husband in everything he did, and their home was often filled with Labor supporters, including Bill Donnelly and Jock Nelson, talking politics. In 1951, Nick decided to nominate for election for Legislative Council for the Batchelor Constituency. In this he had the support of the NT Trades and Labor Council. His opponent was the sitting member, Fred Dowling, also a Labor candidate – albeit unendorsed by the party.

One of Nick's pledges was to fight for the north–south railway that would connect the Territory to South Australia. At a public election meeting held in Katherine on Monday, 23 April 1951, Nick also stated that he 'supported the claim for equal citizens' rights for the coloured population'. He was clearly a man of vision – it wasn't until 1967 that the Aboriginal people of Australia were recognised as citizens and it was to be almost fifty years before the north–south railway was completed when the famous Ghan train made its inaugural journey from Adelaide to Katherine in 2001.

Nick Forscutt was not successful in his campaign, taking 34.3 per cent of the votes, while Fred Dowling maintained his seat with 65.7 per cent. My grandfather was tenacious, though, and decided to stand again in the by-election caused by the resignation of the sitting member, Tom Ronan, in Springvale in April 1955. On that occasion, Nick was endorsed as the Labor Party candidate. His opponent was Harold 'Tiger' Brennan, who stood as an independent and won the seat quite conclusively.

Sadly, my grandfather was to only enjoy thirteen years in the Territory he was so passionate about. He died of a stroke in 1959, at the age of forty-nine, in Katherine.

Around the same time as the Forscutts moved to Katherine, my father, Terry Clements, also arrived in the town, aged twelve. Terry's mother, Lillian Clements, had fled a violent first marriage in country South Australia, taking with her her sons Bob, aged twelve, and Terry, aged six. She found a job working as a cook in a hotel in Adelaide. Bob left Lillian's care to find work when he was fourteen and Terry was subsequently brought up as an only child, cherished, spoilt and protected.

Adelaide was where Lillian met the railway station-master George Tindill, who had been evacuated from Katherine to Adelaide during the war. Following a brief romance and a year of writing letters, Lillian arrived in Katherine to live with George in 1946. During the long-distance romance, Lillian had sent Terry to live with some friends in Broken Hill because there had been an outbreak of the crippling disease poliomyelitis, which could cause high fevers and permanent paralysis, and she was terrified that her young son would catch it. Following her marriage to George in 1947, she brought Terry with her and they lived a happy life in a big old upstairs tropical house right beside the tiny two-room railway station. Lillian, unlike my grandmother Gladys, washed and ironed Terry's clothes and laid them on the bed for him to wear to school every day. She cooked three-course meals for her family, whether it was 100 degrees in the wet season or cold, dry weather, wind cutting through the wooden louvres into the house.

Lillian had a glass cabinet filled with delicate glassware, plastic roses in a dainty ballerina vase, a Bakelite radio and three china ducks flying across the wall. She had hand-crocheted doilies on her dressing table with elegant figurines and a crystal bowl that held marquisite earrings and an opal brooch that I would eventually inherit. (I am sorry that I didn't claim the flying ducks!) Nana Lil was a self-taught dressmaker and she set up a dress shop in the main street called Lillian Frock Shop, which she stocked with ladies dresses and underwear ordered from Adelaide.

Along with other teenagers from Katherine, my mother and father were sent the 1500 kilometres south to Alice Springs for their high schooling. Katherine, a small town of 200 people, did not have a high school. Darwin was only 300 kilometres to the north but didn't have any boarding facilities, which meant that most of the secondary school-age teenagers were sent interstate to boarding schools. Many, though, were sent to Griffith House boarding hostel in Alice Springs, a town with a population that was a hodgepodge of European people – Dutch, German Irish, English – and the Afghans who plied the camel trains carrying stores and mail to remote communities and roadhouses in the desert.

Those girls who did not go away to school went to work at the hospital or one of the local hotels as a house cleaner or nanny. And, reluctantly, my mother soon joined their ranks: she left school in year nine, at fifteen years of age, and returned to Katherine to earn a living. Mum was very good at maths and her first job was working at March Motors Garage as the bookkeeper, as well as pouring petrol at the bowsers.

When Mum returned to Katherine, Terry was sent to Rostrevor College in Adelaide to finish his schooling and on return worked for a year with Mum's brothers, Rex and Bill Forscutt, until he got a job working for the Welfare Department in Alice Springs. My mother went with Terry to Alice Springs, where she worked as a cleaner at the local pub, the Underdowns' hotel, until they were married in March 1955. They were both twenty years of age when they wed; Mum was a five-foot-two Elizabeth Taylor lookalike with dark hair and sapphire blue eyes. Terry was a catch: tall, thin and good looking, with a cheeky smile and a head full of curly blond hair.

I have vague recollections of our time in Alice Springs, living in a low-set grey fibro house with red soil in the front yard and no garden, set against the backdrop of the McDonnell Ranges. I don't have any recollection of a favourite teddy, doll or books, or any reminder of those years other than some lovely photos of my parents' wedding, with Mum's older brother, Uncle Rex, and younger sister, Sue, in the wedding party. I do remember a beautiful lamp in the shape of an African lady with big gold hoop earrings, portrayed in a kneeling position and holding a large orange lampshade, which my mother threw at my father. It smashed.

Dress-up parties were the entertainment of the time and there are photos of Mum and her friends dressed up as Mexicans, Nefertiti and sultans. There are some photos of me at about twelve months old, with beautiful blonde curls (if I may say so), in a big pram wearing a gorgeous little navy and white sailor dress, with a huge white sulphur-crested cockatoo sitting on the edge of the pram. There is also a photo of me with a huge python wrapped around my pram.

My brother Billy was born in December 1957 and my baby sister Shing two years after that, in August 1960. Billy and I slept in the one bed and Shing in a rickety wooden cot. Shing's official name is Kristen; however, she was called 'Little Thing', which became 'Little Shing', and that finally became Shing. Shing was a tiny thing who sucked her thumb and everyone loved her, including me.

Though my parents had nothing and lived in a Housing Commission house, Terry still managed to save enough money to go to the 1956 Melbourne Olympics – on his own; Mum, of course, had to stay behind and look after me. Mum couldn't drive so she walked everywhere with the kids in a pram or relied on taxis to take her shopping or my father to take her out. My vague memory of Terry is that he was soft spoken, easygoing and always happy. He was always immaculately attired for his job at the Welfare Department, wearing the Territory Government dress code of ironed white shirt, tailored grey shorts, long white socks and shiny black shoes. He must have ironed his own shirts because I am pretty sure Mum would not have done it.

One day, Mum just decided that this was not the life she wanted and Terry was not the husband for her, and she left him when I was five years old. I do not think there were any major dramas with my parents' marriage; certainly, I don't remember any, but I was very young. My mother is a passionate woman with a great appetite for and interest in life, and I can only imagine that she didn't much like the prospect of living out her days as an Alice Springs housewife.

I don't remember having any feeling or emotion about the split as my father wasn't around a lot, and I felt totally loved and secure with my mother and my little brother and sister. Nothing much would change about our day-to-day life once we left Terry. Perhaps that is why I don't have strong memories of that time.

It was extremely hard for my mother, aged just twenty-five with three small children, to leave her husband, but she had decided that there was no future for her in the marriage. This was a brave move in 1960, when women were expected to stay in a marriage, no matter how bad or sad. There were no government or welfare benefits to support women if they left. The men controlled all the finances and did not legally have to pay maintenance for their children, so there was no guaranteed financial support there either. Divorce could only be obtained through one of the partners declaring to be at fault, such as having an affair, and most women didn't have the financial resources to hire a lawyer to petition for a divorce. Women were also unable to obtain bank loans unless approved by a husband or a father.

So when Mum separated from Terry, she did not receive any payments to help her with living costs. She had left school at fifteen and hadn't had much experience working before becoming a mother, therefore there wasn't much chance of her getting a job – plus there was the issue of what she'd do with her children while she was working. So the only option for her was to return to live with her mother. Mum packed everything she needed into a couple of suitcases and, along with her three babies, flew the 1200 kilometres north to live with Gladys in Katherine. Mum didn't look back, and we just wanted to be where she was. Besides, there were adventures awaiting us in Katherine and beyond – bigger and better than anything we could ever have imagined.

In our new life, we had to rely on my grandmother for all our food and clothing. Of course, Nana – who was by now a widow supporting her family – wasn't eligible for any kind of support either, so she worked. Typical of my mother and grandmother, neither complained, and in the usual Forscutt family style, everyone chipped in to help.

I loved living with my nana, whose personality was as big and bold as, but maybe a little gentler than, my mother's. The house was full of people coming and going, so there were always extra people at the dinner table and plenty of laughter. Our arrival there began a new journey for all of us.

Chapter 2

NANA'S HOUSE

KATHERINE IS ABOUT 300 KILOMETRES SOUTH-EAST OF Darwin. The area has long been home to the local Jawoyn, Dagoman, Dalabon and Wardaman peoples. Its European history started when an explorer named John McDouall Stuart found himself in the area in 1862 and he named the Katherine River after the daughter of John Chambers, a wealthy South Australian landowner who helped finance his exploration of the north. In the 1960s it was still home to the local Indigenous people and about 300 white people. It was a busy, vibrant town with a dusty main street and a railway station that serviced the massive outback region from the Gulf of Carpentaria to the border with Western

Australia. The town has always owed much of its livelihood
– and its recent history – to the pastoral industry and the
railway.

Katherine's streets are full of the red dirt that is typical
of that part of Australia. It gets on cars and people, and
is embedded into the asphalt on the roads. The red landscape is punctuated by large frangipani trees covered in
deep green leaves and small clusters of blossoms; there are
poincianas with their flame-red flowers and mango trees
laden with their heavy fruit, and lots of other tropical
trees that provide homes and shelter for all sorts of insects
and animals. In the dry season the searing heat of the
day is barely broken at night; in the wet season the whole
region grows lush and heavy with humidity. While I was
growing up there, air conditioning hadn't been invented
and the best we could hope for was a ceiling fan to shift
the air around, if not actually make it cooler. The heat
and humidity were just facts of life and Katherine wouldn't
have been the same without them.

When we moved to Katherine it had a post office and
two pubs, a hospital, police station and church. There
were two garages, Pascoes and March Motors, and two
cafés, Mrs Petersen's and the Sorrento Café, along with
Cox's Store and Katherine Stores, both owned by the Cox
family. There was a picture theatre in the main street
where the white people sat in canvas chairs up the back

and the Aboriginal people sat on a cement slab with their blankets at the front. There was a tin roof over the seated area that leaked buckets of water when it rained, the noise drowning out the sounds of the movie. There was an active branch of the CWA, of which both my grandmothers were president at different times during the 1950s. The women of Katherine enjoyed any chance to get together and celebrate, whether it was Christmas, birthdays, a christening, a funeral, a game of cricket or tennis, or just a Friday night at the club. Both my grandmothers were good friends and enjoyed the social life of the town to its fullest. The CWA fundraised for the school and the community Christmas parties, and catered for a lot of the local events such as dances and weddings as well as helping families in need with food parcels and clothing.

My grandmother had moved from the house at the hot springs to a house in Fourth Street. The factory where my grandmother worked was a huge noisy corrugated-iron shed right next door to her house, at a time when Fourth Street marked the edge of town. Nana's best friends, Henry and Gwendolyn Scott, owned the factory. Nana worked long hours making the fizzy soft drinks that we called lolly water, so we used to say that she worked at the lolly water factory. I thought it was pretty special that Nana worked there, because lolly water was such a treat – and she had access to it every single day.

Nana and Mrs Scott chattered happily over the industrial noise as they loaded the thick cordial base into the machines. They were up on all the town gossip and the latest happenings of the families in the long-running radio serial *Blue Hills*. The bottles rattled along conveyor belts and were filled with bubbling soda water, then topped up with sticky, sweet, coloured syrups. The bottles were then juggled along another large clunking machine where the caps were clamped onto them. They were manually packed into wooden crates and delivered to the local shops. There was sarsaparilla, raspberry, orange, lemonade, lime, creaming soda, banana, pineapple, cola, ginger ale and ginger beer, and large quantities of plain soda water for the local hotels.

The factory later supplied shops with the specially designed soft-drink fridges that allowed you to insert a coin into the slot in the side of the machine to release the cold drink. These were very modern pieces of equipment for a town that didn't have telephones or television. The shops would clean the empty soft-drink bottles, put them into the crates and return them to the factory, where they were placed into vats of caustic soda for a final clean and refilling. In 1969, the lolly water factory was bought from the Scott family by my uncle Jim Forscutt, who expanded the business to supply soft drinks as far away as the mining town of Tennant Creek and the roadhouses of Barry Caves to the south and Adelaide River in the north.

When Nana started working at the factory, my grandfather Nick was still alive, although wheelchair bound after suffering a stroke. Throughout her working day, Nana would regularly go next door to check on him, prepare meals on the wood stove and do all the washing in a blazing copper in the backyard. Nick would have another stroke and die before we moved to Katherine, so I never knew him.

Nana had an Aboriginal couple, Maudie and Smiler, help with the children, washing and keeping the sparse garden. I suppose our arrival in Katherine just meant more people for Nana to look after, as Mum's three younger brothers and sister were there as well as our Great Uncle Bill, plus there were friends, and friends of friends who stayed for up to weeks and months at a time. But we all fitted into the big old Sydney Williams–style corrugated-iron house with its rough cement floors and rickety doors that were never closed. There was plenty of room for everyone at the big wooden kitchen table where we gathered at lunchtime to listen to the ABC radio news and, of course, *Blue Hills*.

My nana's house was pretty basic, with a big hot water donkey out the back of the laundry, where a fire was lit under a 44-gallon drum set on four 'legs' to boil the water for the house. We were always climbing through the woodheap full of snakes for wood to stoke the fire. The bedrooms at one end of the house were separated by curtains strung on fencing wire from steel beams. Large, wispy white mosquito nets flowed over the wrought-iron beds with their bumpy mattresses. The beds were high off the floor and wooden soft-drink crates were kept underneath so we could step up into them.

I hated going to the corrugated iron toilet down the backyard. The toilet itself, made from a cut-out 44-gallon tin drum, was too high for small children, so we had to climb up on to the seat and squat over the hole, which revealed a massive black glob of poo mixed with the magazines and newspapers that were used as toilet paper. In the hot weather the stench was overwhelming. Moreover, the rickety door was heavy and didn't close properly. The tin walls were recycled roofing iron that was dotted with nail holes to peek through and see if anyone was coming. The spider webs rustled around your ears and the toilet creaked in the wind and sighed with the heat. I was terrified of the toilet at night, because I knew that not only were there snakes, lizards, frogs and goannas but a boogie man, who would abduct me for sure. There seemed to be boogie men everywhere in Katherine, as my little friends and I were always hiding from them under the beds in the house or when playing games in the huge mango trees.

It was a happy, rowdy house where my teenage uncle and aunt and their friends practised rock 'n' roll dancing to a bumpy record player in the lounge room. The rough, pitted cement floor did not deter them from rehearsing their routines over and over. I thought Aunty Sue was a movie star with her gorgeous blonde hair, as she twirled in her large skirts and little pumps under Uncle Jim's arms and around his body; changing direction in the blink of an eye, she slipped under his legs and spun around and around, skirts swishing up to her thighs. Uncle Jim was a lovable, boisterous and bumptious character and he called my grandmother 'Tango' when he was in a cheeky mood. He sang a good tune and loved to belt out the latest Marty Robbins or Slim Dusty song.

There was never a dull moment on Fourth Street for me, Billy or Shing. There were so many people in the house that at times it felt as though we were being raised by a village – and we liked it that way. It was good for Mum, too, to have lots of people around to help with us kids. If she ever had a moment of missing our father we would never have known.

The first time I saw Bill Tapp I was five years old and he was standing in the doorway of my grandmother's house.

He was hard to miss: he stood six feet and two inches, sported a big black moustache and a ten-gallon hat, dark moleskin trousers, a deep-blue long-sleeved RM Williams shirt and high-heeled riding boots. Around his hips he had two leather belts – one a bull strap for catching wild bulls and the other a bandolier with a row of silver bullets – and a black Luger pistol jutting out of a holster, just like in the cowboy movies.

No wonder my mother fell for him straightaway.

It was 1960 and Bill Tapp had come to town with my two uncles – who worked for him at Killarney Station. They invited him to stay with them at my grandmother's house whenever he was in town. 'Hello, M-M-Mrrrsss F-F-F-Forscutt,' Bill Tapp would stutter in his deep voice. He always called her 'M-M-Mrrrsss F-F-F-Forscutt' no matter how many times she said, 'Oh, Bill, for goodness' sake, call me Glad.'

Katherine did not have a motel or boarding hostel at that time, so anyone who was visiting town had to find someone to stay with. More often than not, it seemed, that someone was Nana. She always had a meal and a bed out the back for the boarders who would come and stay for a week or a month – or longer, as in the case of old Doug Hudspeth, carpenter at the Katherine Hospital and a piano player, who arrived after my grandfather died and never left until his own death twenty years later. Doug and Nana settled into a happy relationship and I remember Doug as a happy-go-lucky man who always had a beer in his hand. Doug promised to marry Nana and make her an honest woman but Nana was not interested and regularly said she was happy to be the 'scarlet woman'. However, Doug insisted that he buy her a gold wedding band when they went to visit his family in New South Wales in the 1970s, to 'keep up appearances'.

Born Charles William Tapp in Sydney in June 1929, Bill Tapp was the only child of Sarah Ann and Ernest Charles Tapp. He grew up a pampered only child and although his mother adored him, she was a woman of her time – distant from him emotionally, although she turned herself inside out trying to give him a good life and help him succeed. Bill grew up in the prestigious eastern suburb of Vaucluse, which hugs Sydney Harbour close to the end of South Head. The Tapps lived in a grand, sprawling house with a tennis court and a housekeeper – and Bill Tapp never lost his taste for the finer things in life. He attended a private school, The Scots College, in nearby Bellevue Hill. In his senior years at school Bill Tapp became a full-time boarder, as his father was ill with cancer and his mother travelled overseas on buying trips for the upmarket homewares company Rosenthal. Bill Tapp was good at everything he applied himself to, representing his school in swimming, rowing, cricket, boxing and football. He played tennis with Australian champions Ken Rosewall, Lew Hoad and Frank Sedgman during his school years. Though tall and good looking as a teenager, and accomplished at so many things, self-confidence was not one of Bill Tapp's strong points. He was painfully shy and the severe stutter that was evident when we met him in Katherine would plague him all his life.

His lifelong schoolfriend was David Brockhoff, who went on to become one of Australia's great rugby union identities, playing eight Tests as flanker between 1949 and 1951. He also coached the Australian team for several years in the 1970s.

Dave and his wife, Claire, came to visit Killarney a number of times with their family. I interviewed Dave in Sydney just after Bill Tapp's death. He spoke about Bill Tapp's sporting prowess, his natural talent for any sport he participated in. He said that he was a charismatic person, good looking and popular, but that his shyness and stutter completely inhibited his social life.

Bill Tapp's life in the Northern Territory was at complete odds with his upbringing. It began as an idea when, as a teenager, he read the book *The Cattle King* by Ion L Idriess, the story of Sir Sidney Kidman, who had started with almost nothing after running away from home at the age of thirteen and ended up owning an empire of cattle stations across the north of Australia. Although Bill Tapp had a privileged life, there was clearly something about Kidman's story that clicked with him. Most of his school holidays were spent with his school mates who had cattle and horse properties in country New South Wales. A friend from those days whom I had contact with after Bill Tapp's death told me that as a teenager from the city, Bill Tapp immediately had a rapport with the animals and quickly became a good horseman and confident in handling the livestock.

He wrote to his mother from boarding school, telling her that he wanted to leave Sydney as soon as he finished school to go to the Northern Territory. By chance, his mother had met a Mr HE Thonemann, who owned the sprawling, isolated cattle property Elsey Station in the Northern Territory, near the tiny township of Mataranka, 400 kilometres south of Darwin; Elsey Station was made famous by Jeannie Gunn in her book, *We of the Never Never*. Sarah Tapp was able to secure young Bill a job as a jackaroo, starting at Elsey Station in the dry season of 1947, the same year my mother came to the Territory as a twelve-year-old.

Bill Tapp's father, Ernest, died in 1947, and Bill Tapp left Sydney soon after, at the age of seventeen, to take up his position as jackaroo-bookkeeper. He soon settled into station life, learning everything he could, and the manager

Bill Crowson and his wife, Violet, took young Bill Tapp under their wing.

Bill Tapp said in later years that when he arrived at Elsey Station he found it difficult to reconcile his position as a white man living alongside Aboriginal people who dwelled in humpies and were dished out limited rations and tobacco, with no access to toilets, showers or a laundry to wash their clothes, and who were not invited to eat anywhere near the white people. He'd never experienced anything like it and he didn't like the injustice of it. Though he lived in only slightly better conditions, a shed when in at the station and swags most of the time, as far as he was concerned the Aboriginal people were no different to him.

Over the course of his time at Elsey Station, Bill Tapp developed a close relationship with the Crowsons – so much so that a few years after he arrived, they all went together to manage Rosewood Station on the Northern Territory–Western Australia border. After two years at Rosewood Station they left to establish their own droving business. Bill Crowson was the boss drover and he and Bill Tapp made a number of trips together in the early 1950s, moving cattle from Alice Springs through Tennant Creek and Elliott and along the Murranji Track. The Murranji, one of the most notoriously treacherous stock routes in the Northern Territory, was known for its long distances between water holes through hot, dry lancewood country.

The drovers needed to have an intricate knowledge of the distances, the pace they could push the cattle and what water holes would still have water by the end of the dry season.

In 1952, Bill Tapp and Bill Crowson formed a partnership and, with financial assistance from Sarah Tapp, bought Montejinni Station, formerly part of Victoria River Downs Station and over 600 kilometres south of Darwin, based on their ability to fulfil the required covenants in a government tender system. The covenants were a legal requirement and this included having to supply a minimum number of water bores and to build a set number of miles of fencing and access roads to ensure the properties developed and became productive. In the early years of the twentieth century, Victoria River Downs (VRD) had been owned by Sidney Kidman and the federal government had excised the properties of Camfield, Montejinni and Killarney from it in order to encourage development and settlement in the area.

At the time of the purchase, Bill Tapp and the Crowsons were living in the tiny town of Elliott, a remote place on the Stuart Highway where Violet Crowson worked as the postmistress, while they waited to hear if their tender for the property was successful. As soon as they received the news that it was, the trio packed up and left. Bill and Violet Crowson drove the truck, packed with their children and all their worldly goods, up the Murranji to Montejinni. Bill Tapp walked their horses the 500 kilometres to the new station, in company with some Aboriginal stockmen and a sixteen-year-old deaf man, Kenny Wesley. At the same time, Paul Vandeleur and his brother Mick had successfully acquired Camfield Station, and Eric Izod and Ivor Townshend Hall drew Killarney Station.

The partnership went well for the first few years but began to develop cracks. As the relationship deteriorated Bill Tapp cast his eye around the region looking for an opportunity to buy his own property with no partners; he heard that the neighbouring station of Killarney was up for sale and started talks with the owners, Eric Izod and Ivor Townshend Hall, about buying Killarney. In 1960, he reached an agreement to pay £90 000, a record price for a Northern Territory cattle station at that time.

Thirteen years after arriving in the Northern Territory as a teenage jackaroo, thirty-year-old Bill Tapp moved onto his own cattle station. This gave him the freedom to implement and develop his own ideas and dreams – his transformation into a Territory cattle king was now underway. The signing over of the property was a protracted affair but this did not stop Bill Tapp from working day and night, mustering and building fences to contain the wild cattle. He finally received the title to Killarney in 1962.

Bill Tapp's empire began under a bough shed at Mayvale Bore on Killarney. He led a frugal life, working with a stock camp that consisted of my teenage uncles, Jimmy and Boko Forscutt; Joey and Alfie Russell; and Kenny Wesley. They slept in swags, moving around the station with pack horses carrying their swags, shoeing and fencing gear and all the supplies, their food – flour, salted beef, sugar and tea. They rarely went to town or indulged in luxuries such as a warm shower or a beer.

Bill Tapp told my uncles that he fell in love with my mother the first day he saw her, and that he was going to marry her. He was thirty-one years old by then and he had never had a relationship with a woman – which was hardly a surprise, given the life he'd been leading: there weren't many unmarried women to be found on the cattle stations of the Northern Territory.

Years later I would ask my mother what she thought of Bill Tapp after that first meeting at her mother's house. She said that she thought he was 'a bit peculiar'. He was shy and stuttered badly; she also noticed that he was quiet and gentle. Within a few hours she'd also picked up that he was extremely concerned about cruelty or harm to insects and animals. 'His mind was to give him no rest from his obsessions,' she said.

But they were able to laugh together and Bill Tapp wouldn't go away – he kept coming to Katherine to see

Mum. She said that, looking back on it all, 'I should have run a mile, but I was newly out of a marriage, with no money and in strange circumstances, and I was in love.'

Their relationship developed quickly over a very short time. Bill Tapp's idea of courting was to take Mum to the river and show off his diving skills by doing swan dives and backflips off the Low Level bridge into the Katherine River while us kids paddled around in the shallows. He was a man of few words and didn't say much to us; however, I immediately liked and trusted him because I felt the intense love that he had for my mother. He also liked Nana and her no-nonsense family, who were some of the few who could draw him out of his shyness with a good joke and a big laugh. He seemed keen to take on the whole package of a ready-made family and didn't interfere with our lives too much. We had a big extended family around us and lots of new little friends in the neighbourhood. I felt secure and happy in my life, and I am sure Billy and Shing felt the same. We had no reason to worry about anything – we had family and fun every day of our lives, and we were well taken care of. Bill Tapp was just another interesting element in a full life.

Before long, Bill Tapp asked my mother to go out to Killarney with him. He wanted to marry her. The fact that Mum was still legally married to Terry Clements didn't seem to deter either of them and within six months, in

1961, we were making plans to drive the 270 kilometres to Killarney.

As far as Billy and I were concerned, this was just another adventure. Shing was far too young to know what was going on, and even if she had, she just would have gone along with it. The three of us were a little pack and we would follow Mum wherever she went. All that mattered to me was that Mum was happy and we were all together. We were leaving Nana and her boisterous household behind but she wouldn't be far away. A new life was waiting for us down a road that we would come to travel many times over the next few years.

Chapter 3

WELCOME TO KILLARNEY

WHEN MY MOTHER ASKED BILL TAPP WHAT SHE NEEDED to take for her first trip out to his cattle station, he replied with a shy grin, 'Oh, don't worry, we have everything we need.'

In her excitement at going bush and living in a real homestead, my mother packed only the necessities: a small suitcase of clothing, tins of powdered milk and baby bottles, Weet-bix, tins of Heinz baked beans and spaghetti, and lots of nappies. Mum was cautious but also head over heels in love with Bill Tapp and prepared to take on whatever was waiting for her at this strange new place. She never thought about the consequences of what she was doing; she never considered that life at Killarney might be considerably different to life in Katherine. She's always been pretty adventurous. Her family had taken that first big adventure to Katherine – her mother's marriage had taken her on another adventure so Mum may have considered that she was doing the same thing; she wasn't going as far as her mother had, but she was still striking out in search of something new and hopefully better.

On that first trip to Killarney we travelled all day. It was a hot, dusty drive over scratchy dirt tracks, up rocky ridges, down dry creeks and across black soil plains; my mother and the man she had fallen in love with, cramped with three children under the age of six in the front seat of a smoke-blowing, engine-roaring Bedford truck.

The miles crept slowly by; we pulled over periodically for a toilet stop, to stretch our legs and have a drink of water before finally arriving beside a creaking windmill and rusty water tank just as the sun was going down. After almost 300 kilometres of road, Mum crawled out of the truck, exhausted, and let the children out to have a run around.

'How much further do we have to go?' she asked Bill Tapp.

'Oh, this is it,' he proudly declared as he pointed to a bough shed with no walls and an open fire surrounded by black pots and pans. Mum stared in amazement at her new home: a rickety shed made of six wooden posts with dried branches layered over the top for a roof and an ominous hand-painted sign, 'COCKRAG DOWNS' – the meaning of cockrag being 'broken down and uncared for'. It was also the name used for a piece of rag that the Aboriginal men used to wrap through their legs and tie on each side, in a nappy style, for dancing corroboree.

There wasn't much else at Killarney besides that shed; the area around Mayvale Bore was almost devoid of trees, as they'd presumably been cut down by the previous occupants for use as firewood. The ground was dry, and the flat red landscape was dotted with millions of ant hills, scrawny trees and stumpy yellow grass as far as the eye could see. And out there, somewhere, were cattle. It was Bill Tapp's blank canvas, and he had dreams of filling it with proper cattle yards, camp buildings and a homestead. That vision was still in his head, though – all we could see was that almost empty area around the shed, and beyond that the bare land stretching away on all sides.

When Mum asked Bill Tapp where the toilet was, he said, 'Down the creek.' So she duly set off on foot with Billy, Shing and me, looking for a lone tin shed. After quite a trek with no sign of anything that looked like a toilet except the odd scattering of newspaper and toilet paper littered along the dry riverbed, she realised that the 'toilet' was to squat behind the biggest tree you could find.

Bill Tapp had told Mum that 'everything they needed' was at Killarney but what he really meant was 'everything a man needed' – that is, swags under a tree, and plenty of beef, flour, sugar and black tea. There was a large open fire with buckets of water and cast-iron camp ovens simmering away on the coals – for cooking and, when needed, for keeping warm – and a massive woodheap full of insects and snakes. Damper (made from flour, baking powder, salt and water), large legs of roast beef, and stews were cooked in those camp ovens, which were put in a hole in the ground with hot stones placed in the bottom and hot coals on the top. The billycans – which bubbled day and night with thick black tea – and the camp ovens were moved about by cooking utensils that were shaped out of fencing wire. There was no house, no running water or refrigeration, no toilet or fresh food or vegetables. My mother might not have been used to living in luxury but she had never lived in the open before – let alone subjected her children to such conditions.

Mum could not drive, though, so there was no turning back for her or us. She had made her decision to be with Bill Tapp and she just had to get on with living on Killarney in conditions that would make most other women flee. She quickly learnt to sleep in a swag on the ground, to do the washing in cut-off 44-gallon drums and bathe the three of us in tin buckets behind the water tank. We soon adapted to having no proper toilet – when you're a little kid such a thing isn't a big deal – although it was no fun when the all-too-regular sharp pains of impending dysentery bolted through my gut and I had to make a dash for the nearest tree.

That bough shed was the kitchen, the office and doctor's surgery all at once. Communications with the outside world were conducted on a Codan two-way radio that was powered by a twelve-volt battery. The radio sat on a rusty 5-gallon drum under a tree with its wire aerial thrown into the branches in search of patchy reception. The 'scheds' – scheduled sessions; the times to send telegrams and order food, stores and mechanical parts for the station, to have inter-station discussions with neighbours, buy and sell cattle, or talk to the doctor – were transferred through Radio Victor Juliet Yankee (VJY) from Wyndham in Western Australia, three times a day. Most of the time the radio was crackly and indecipherable but everyone knew everyone's business anyway. Announcements of births, marriages and deaths were also transmitted across the airwaves.

Things that wouldn't have made sense to people who lived in houses, in towns, made perfect sense to us. It didn't occur to me that it was strange that we weren't sleeping inside the shed. It was more important, and logical, that the food not get wet than that we didn't get wet. We always had to think about the survival of the bigger organism that was Killarney; there was no point keeping the people dry if the flour was wet and couldn't be used to make damper.

Because there was no refrigeration, our diet was basic and monotonous – we couldn't have stored perishable fruit and vegetables, let alone anything more exotic like cheese, even if we could get hold of it. Instead there was plenty of tough beef to eat: fried, grilled, salted, stewed and roasted; and the stores consisted of tinned Sunshine milk, bags of sugar, cartons of loose tea leaves, flour, salt and baking powder, along with soap and tobacco. Most vegetables came out of tins, and there were the occasional tins of salted butter, jam, peaches and apricots. There was no special cooking for kids – or anyone. We all ate the same thing, which was beef, and there were always lots of big stews, so I guess that was the soft food for the kids. All the little kids chewed on rib bones for their teething rings.

Most of the fresh beef was corned – that is, covered in coarse salt and laid out on an old wire bed frame to dry, the same process that these days produces beef jerky. This was our staple diet, interspersed with fresh steak and rib bones when we got a 'killer' – a steer that was to be killed for food – every week. The meat hung under the bough shed on wire hooks, covered in black flies, the blood dripping onto the ground. The fresh and corned beef was regularly supplemented by freshly killed bush turkey and goanna.

The beef was mostly accompanied by the staple vegetables of pumpkin, potato and onion – because they were the only vegetables that survived without refrigeration – followed by slabs of damper and tins of thick, bittersweet treacle for dessert. Curry powder was the only spice available and was mostly used to cover the taste of rotting beef that had green stuff growing around the edges. Everything was cooked in lashings of fat, salt and sugar.

All meals were eaten off enamelled plates while sitting on the ground around the fire at night or under the trees during the day. The sole table was a discarded wooden door placed on top of two empty 44-gallon drums. This table was used to prepare food, store the rations off the ground and discourage the ants. All the dry goods were kept in 4-gallon tin drums to keep the weather out, but they were not very useful at keeping the weevils and bugs at bay. The coarse salt and sugar came in plastic-lined hessian bags – that set like a rock in the hot humid weather – and had to be broken and crushed into small pieces with a horse-shoeing hammer.

It wasn't all meat and veg, though – we ate plenty of bush tucker supplied by the Aboriginal people who also lived on Killarney: wild bananas and oranges, bush potatoes, paddy melons, the wild honey known as 'sugar-bag' and juicy purple conkerberries. However, the harshness of that first year affected us all. There was a severe shortage of food and we went for months without milk or vegetables and lived on sweet black tea and lots of fresh and salted beef.

There was no electricity or running water, no telephones, radio or television, so when we weren't tearing about the place we entertained ourselves with storytelling, guitars and music – we were never bored. My mother was reliant on drovers travelling through the area to bring supplies of powdered milk, tinned vegetables and the most treasured items: old newspapers, magazines and books. Mum was a prolific reader and read most of the world's classics thanks to what the drovers gave to her. She would say that she knew the instructions on the milk and jam tins off by heart because there was nothing else to read. Bill Tapp loved to read *Queensland Country Life* and *Phantom* comics. He religiously kept a diary and journalled the wages and stores in a red hardcover book.

There were about fifteen people living on the outstation at this time. Because there was no housing, everyone camped under humpies or tarpaulins strung between trees. The Aboriginal families who lived on Killarney were mainly Mutburra people, with interfamily connections to the Gurindji people of Wave Hill. One of the Aboriginal women, Dora, lived under a humpy with her daughter Nita, who was a couple of years older than me, while another woman, Daisy, and her husband, Banjo – who was Dora's son – camped just a short way from them. The single Aboriginal men, Georgie and Cloud, camped further away under another tree. The white stockmen, including my uncles Jim and Boko, camped with their mates from Katherine, Alfie and Joe Russell, and Kenny Wesley, in another group, further away from the women.

My mother, Bill Tapp and we three kids slept in open swags under our chandelier of stars. Our swags were thin, itchy, grey army blankets and the pillows were made of the sum total of our clothing rolled into a little bundle. I never minded sleeping rough. It was just normal – everyone else was sleeping in a swag, so it didn't occur to me to miss the bed I'd known in Nana's house in Katherine. Under the Milky Way we held competitions to see who was the first to spot the Evening Star, who was the first to find a satellite floating steadily across the galaxy and who saw the first sliver of moon break onto the southern horizon. From a very young age, I could identify the Southern Cross and Orion with his belt and scabbard. I loved the full-moon nights when the shadows of the trees turned into scary monsters with which I could create stories of monsters and boogie men to frighten my younger siblings. On moonless nights we curled up with the blankets over our heads in case those boogie men came to get us. During the wet season we shared our shelter – an upturned water tank – with spiders and snakes all trying to get out of the rain.

I was happy, gathering around the open campfire for breakfast and dinner with Mum and Bill Tapp and the stockmen, and running wild with my brother Billy in between. The men went mustering all day, so while they were gone there was mostly just my mother, and Daisy and Dora, who entertained us with songs and stories and took us hunting for bush tucker. All the kids were burnt brown as we ran around in pants with no shoes or shirts. Our knotted hair was full of nits. It was a very free way of living – not everyone's cup of tea, but it kept things simple: if we didn't wear clothes there weren't clothes to get dirty, so Mum didn't have to wash as much.

Mum recalls that first year at Killarney as being tough without any facilities and living around a camp fire and constantly worrying about the lack of water, but she never thought of leaving.

Mum's brother Boko (real name Francis) had started working for Bill Tapp just before Bill Tapp met my mother, and he continued to live and work at Killarney after Mum moved there. He was a lovable larrikin who sang and laughed a lot. On one occasion after a drinking session at the nearby roadhouse at Top Springs – an outback service station, pub and store – Boko returned very happily drunk and jumped on Bill Tapp's horse, which was saddled and waiting under a shady tree. He pulled the Luger rifle out of the saddle holster and fired a few shots into the air, just as if he was in a John Wayne movie, setting 500 head of cattle into a panic as they scattered and galloped through our camp.

The cattle trampled over swags and through the camp fires, knocking over billycans and tables of food. Mum and Daisy and Dora were running, screaming, and dragging all the kids behind trees, while the stockmen were galloping up and down the creek trying to get the cattle under control. When the stampede was over, the camp looked like a cyclone had gone through it and everyone was fuming.

Bill Tapp dragged Boko off the horse by the scruff of the neck and gave him a good dressing down, saying how people could have been trampled to death, not to mention they now had to muster half the mob of cattle still galloping in terror across the plains.

Boko was a little sedate for a few days but it was not long before his mischievous personality returned and he continued to be the life of the camp.

Having Boko and our other uncle, Jimmy, around made Killarney seem like it wasn't so different to Nana's house in Katherine – it was just a bigger, more rugged version with no walls and no windows. We also had the family of the camp – not just our uncles but the other stockmen, as well as the Aboriginal families who lived with us. Everyone lived the same way, under the same conditions, and everyone had a role to play in the running of the camp. The kids got to be kids for a while, but not forever – there would be jobs for us, too, eventually. In the meantime, we could run wild and have fun; we could learn about the land and what it could provide us with; we'd live through the seasons and learnt how they affected everyone. Basically, for me I just lived each day as it came. This was not the case for Bill Tapp, who was constantly planning more paddocks to control the cattle, more access into the scrub country, more water bores and income to pay for the stores, vehicle and repairs. For the rest of us, we didn't think about the next day. We couldn't – we didn't know what the next day would bring. It was a way of life that kept things simple. It was a way of life that, as a still-small child, I learnt to love.

Chapter 4

DAISY AND DORA

BEFORE WE MOVED TO KILLARNEY, A PASSING DROVER had told Bill Tapp about a small group of Aboriginal people walking around the country who were looking for work. They were living in the scrub, away from their homelands, because no one would give them a job. Bill Tapp went looking for the group at Victoria River Downs Station. The Aboriginal people at VRD told him where he would find them, and eventually he tracked down the small family and offered them a job on Killarney.

Banjo Long, who was known to be a good cattleman, had gotten the reputation of being a wild warrior who had killed a couple of Aboriginal men in inter-clan feuds, and had assaulted a white police officer from Timber Creek when they attempted to arrest him. He was a big, good-looking man; dark, quiet and serious. He was known as the Rain Man because he could sing for rain. His wife, Daisy, was a large, cuddly lady with voluminous breasts and a very sweet personality. His brother Georgie was wire thin and agile with a lovely wide smile; he was always happy. Georgie made boomerangs, woomeras and long spears with deadly ironwood points. He loved to show off his boomerang-throwing skills by setting up a flour drum as a target for his practice. He performed the exquisite moves of the brolga and kangaroo dances and did all sorts of birdcalls. He taught me how to blow a leaf and make songs as we rode along behind mobs of cattle.

Old Dora, Banjo's mum, was the boss woman in the camp. We called her Mum and everyone else called her 'Old Dora'. She was a small, round lady who had one deformed foot with three funny little toes bunched together. She wrapped a big bundle of rags, torn grey blankets and a hessian bag around the foot to build it up. The bundle of old rags and blankets was held together with a long piece of cord wrapped around and around the bag. The cord was made from strips of fabric torn from old dresses, knotted together and rolled in goanna fat to give it strength. Dora got about easily on her bag foot, as we called it, and could keep up with the strongest of us as we walked up and down creek beds and across rocky ridges. The crippled foot never slowed her down and it was a sad day many years later when a white doctor from Darwin decided, in his wisdom, to amputate it. Dora, a strong and wiry traditional woman who had walked the length and breadth of the Northern Territory and who had given birth to ten children, declined very quickly after that terrible operation. She had a stroke and died, curled up and speechless.

In her time on Killarney, though, Dora was a cranky old bugger who ruled the camp with her tongue and a nulla-nulla, a type of fighting stick. She was the oldest person in her small group and did not have a husband when she came to Killarney – although she must have had one once, given that she had ten children. Old Dora's word was law and I never saw anyone attempt to challenge her, even her big, strong and much-feared son, Banjo.

Dora kept the law. She taught us the order of Aboriginal society according to skin names and relationships. Skin names are a complicated system created by Aboriginal people over the millennia to ensure that there are no close family bloodline marriages within the small tribes. Dora took us into her family and we took her family into ours. She gave my mother a tribal skin name of the Mutburra and Gurindji people, Nunaku, which made them sisters. Through these skin names we were Dora's children, which made Banjo and his brother Georgie my brothers. My skin name (and my sisters') is Ngunnarryi and the boys are Djungarri. I became proficient in speaking Pidgin English smattered with the local Mutburra and Gurindji dialect and a library full of useful swear words. Dora also painted us with ochre and taught us dances and songs. She told us about the Dreaming and drew animal tracks and stories in the dirt. She taught us all about bush tucker and medicine.

Daisy was about the same age as Dora. We called her 'Buggadu', Gurindji language for 'auntie' or 'sister-in-law'; because Banjo was our brother, we had to call Daisy 'sister-in-law', even though she was old enough to be our grandmother. The young girl relatives on Killarney were not allowed to look at or talk to Banjo or Georgie, as was the traditional practice through the skin system in which the Aboriginal women are not allowed to interact with their brothers or speak their names aloud.

Everyone liked Daisy; she was kind and gentle and never rocked the boat. She sang corroboree songs in a high, sweet voice and told us stories about the Dreaming that coexisted with and ruled their day-to-day lives. Daisy did all the work because she was Dora's daughter-in-law. She prepared the food: rib bones, goanna and little johnnycakes, a type of flat bread made with flour, baking powder, salt and water, pummelled into a flat round cake and cooked on the open coals. She cooked beautiful golden loaves of bread in camp ovens and made brooms out of bushes tied to a long stick to rake the ground around the camp. She did the washing and made huge dresses and petticoats out of cheap floral material, sewing in tiny running stitch with black cotton.

At one stage, Old Daisy became suspicious of Banjo's absences. She finally caught him indulging in clandestine meetings with a pretty young woman called Sarah, in the early hours of the morning at the saddle shed. Stripping down to her fighting clothes, a floral petticoat and red rag tied around her head, and white symbols painted on her long, swaying breasts, she confronted Sarah, screaming and cursing from the humpy she lived in with Banjo, waving her nulla-nulla in the air as she proceeded across the black soil flat towards the cattle yards and Sarah.

Banjo stood to one side, away from Sarah – who was dressed in a blue dress with a white Peter Pan collar that my mother had given her – as though he had played no part in the predicament. Sarah did not move because she knew that she must accept the punishment. Daisy approached swiftly, beating Sarah across the back and legs as the young woman screamed and ducked away from the swinging stick. The beating was cruel but did not break any bones. Daisy gave Sarah a good flogging because it was important for Daisy to save face and give Sarah the appropriate amount of punishment, so that Daisy could maintain her position in the tribe. Banjo's position did not change and he maintained his leadership in their family group. Sarah soon disappeared from the camp to another community.

———

We kids would play under the overflow of the tank and make mud pies while the old women bathed in a cut-off petrol drum behind the water tank. They did their washing at the same time and hung it on a barbed-wire fence to dry. They wore handmade half-slips and their breasts hung free. They had deep tribal scars on their upper arms and they painted lines and circle symbols on their long breasts with white ochre. All of this seemed normal to me: it was how they lived and it was what I grew up with. Daisy and Dora bathed, oiled their skin and wore their best dresses and scarves when they went down to the corrugated-tin store that my mother ran. They collected rations of flour, tea, sugar, salt, treacle and black chewing tobacco, and carried everything home tied in a strip of cloth.

During the Dry, the old women often took us down the creek hunting. Daisy and Dora led the way across the black soil plain to the creek with a bundle of tools for hunting. Dora would hobble along with her bundle of clothes slung across her shoulder and a long walking stick to prod into goanna and lizard holes. The stick was also good for probing into holes in tree trunks for sugar-bag and looking for birds' eggs high up in their nests. Daisy sometimes carried a long stick with a burning coal on the end to start the fire for lunch; she would blow on the coal to keep it burning. But most of the time she started the fire by rubbing two sticks together over a little pile of dry, scrunched-up grass.

We went on our hunting trips well prepared, everyone loaded up with billycans, tea, sugar, flour, treacle and coarse salt. We took a piece of dry corned beef or raw rib bones covered in a greasy bit of rag, ants crawling over it and complemented by a thick layer of black flies hanging around, just in case we couldn't find some other form of protein. We would race ahead of the old ladies, jumping from rock to rock, screeching and squealing in delight, looking for lizard eggs and goanna holes. Dora and Daisy followed, keeping a sharp eye on us. We'd race madly to the conkerberry tree with its juicy red berries that turned our tongues purple; to the wild orange, which we called 'coolinyukka', its fruit the size of a golf ball with a soft red–orange centre, and bush bananas hanging from a vine. There was always a good supply of little dry berries called 'dog's balls' and the small wild onion known as 'brolga tucker'.

We would dig around the edge of billabongs for white ochre because the women needed it to paint themselves. We'd squish the mud through our fingers below the water line, where we could feel the hard clumps in the mud. The white ochre would then be wrapped in a piece of old rag and used for corroborees. The yellow and orange sandstone rock ochre would be ground between two stones then bitten off in small chunks and broken down in the mouth with saliva, to make a smooth paste for body painting or decorating didgeridoos, boomerangs, coolamons and nulla-nullas.

Dora and Daisy made us our own special little coolamons and billycans to carry what we found. The adult billycans were made out of milk tins and our little ones were made out of jam tins. They made us steel digging sticks, shaped in the fire and pounded with a rock to give a flat, bladed end. I would dig away proudly, making little piles of fresh wild potatoes on a coolamon – a shovel-shaped small tree trunk carved from the chitwood tree, used to carry everything from firewood to food and babies – to be cooked in the coals for lunch or taken home for the evening meal. They were the yummiest, though, when they were raw.

In one part of the creek there was a massive wild fig tree laden with plump brown fruit. We would gather these in billycans and if you ate too many you could find yourself spending a lot of time squatting behind a tree with a big bellyache. The gum trees oozed sticky clear gum that hardened into balls on the bark and we chewed on the rather bland white goo that looked and tasted like hardened glue. The bloodwood tree's crystallised red sap was kept in an old tobacco tin and mixed with hot water to use as dysentery medicine.

The favourite tucker for us sweet-toothed bush kids was sugar-bag, wild golden honey that could be spotted by the little black bush bees hovering around a buzzing hole in a tree branch. We would climb the tree and scoop the honey out of the hole with a stick, twisting it around like a lollipop, filling the billycans and licking dripping honey from our hands. The wax from the sugar-bag was stored in milk tins to shape the mouthpieces of didgeridoos.

Whenever we set off with Daisy and Dora it seemed like we walked hundreds of miles from home; later, when I was older, I looked at the area and realised it was only about 3 or 4 kilometres. It would just take us all morning to zigzag our way to the dinner camp under a tree in the dry riverbed.

The ancient paperbark trees and the winding creek bed were our playground. At home in familiar and safe surroundings we played barefoot, soles toughened like elephant skin, racing up and down the creek, climbing trees, mustering cattle on stick horses and waving stick guns. We were dirty and browned by the sun, bursting with excitement and energy, inquisitive about everything in our environment, around every corner, in every tree or under every rock. On each adventure there was sure to be surprise – a goanna, snake or lizard, and, on the odd occasion, a scrub bull or thirsty cow to scare the living daylights out of us.

All the activity centred around the fire and the bottomless billycan of tea simmering on the hot coals. As the old women made johnnycakes and dug a hole to cook the wild yams, we kids would be clambering all around the riverbed, swinging out of trees, laughing and playing imaginary games. We never went too far, though, because Dora had warned us that there were devils and wild dingoes that carried little children away. She would call out along the riverbed, 'Don't go too far. That debil debil gonna get you!'

When lunch was ready we would settle in the shade with a pannikin of sweet black tea, which had its own special pungent taste, from the battered billycan; a billycan had to be leaking before it was replaced, as the tea never tasted as good in a shiny new tin. With bellies full of bush tucker, we would settle down in the midday heat to rest on a mattress of fresh gum leaves. I loved to snuggle against Daisy's belly and drag on the smells of goanna fat and fire overlaid with Sunlight soap in her dress.

In the stillness, the old ladies would tell us stories about the spirits. The women drew pictures of animals and spirits in the sand while telling their stories. They told us about the debil debils in the hills who took naughty children with them, away from their families so they would never be seen again. The most terrifying stories were about the Kadaitcha Man, who roamed day and night across the country. The Kadaitcha Man was magical and knew who was breaking the law – mostly it was those who indulged in marital indiscretions or who disobeyed the elders. He could come in the darkest of nights and remove your kidney fat with his bare hands, leaving no scars, and you would pine away, stop eating and die. It was a sad, lonely death – people knew that you had been 'sung' and you would be excommunicated from the family because of the curse.

These stories kept us in line, as they were designed to do. We would never have dreamt of being cheeky or answering back for fear of the spirits. The stories were endless: family, animals, spirits, and debil debils. There were songs about the stories and Daisy and Dora sang these as we settled down after lunch for a rest. The repetitious droning of the songs wrapped around the trees and travelled along the dry riverbed with the layers of white smoke, sending us to sleep.

When the little ones slept, the women scratched through their hair for nits, crunching the live ones between their teeth or thumbnails. 'Ooohhhh, you got proper big ones,' they would laugh, placing the squirming nits into a tobacco tin to be counted when they were finished.

As the sun headed deep into the west we would have one last play in the afternoon coolness before putting the fire out and covering it with dirt. The leftover food was carried in the coolamon or wrapped in a square piece of rag and hauled over our shoulders. Everyone had something to carry, from the day's harvest of bush tucker to the billycan of sugar-bag, a tomahawk, or a nice, straight piece of tree branch ready to be carved into a fighting stick or coolamon. We would head off home, eyes peeled for the evening meal – hopefully a big, juicy goanna meandering its way into the creek for an evening drink.

If a goanna was sighted, the attack was like a scene out of a 1960s cowboys-and-Indians movie, where we circled the animal, yelling and waving sticks. The sight and sound of Dora brandishing a big nulla-nulla in the air, screaming at the tops of her lungs – 'Git 'em that one, go dat way, come back 'ere' – was enough to give anyone a heart attack, let alone the poor unsuspecting goanna. We kids would all be jumping and squealing with excitement, adding to the cacophony of the kill, adrenaline pumping and hearts racing. Though both Daisy and Dora were big women, they moved with agility, breasts slapping against their chest while clubbing the terrified creature to death.

As the goanna lay lifeless on the hot ground, Daisy would swoop in with glee, pick it up with one hand and haul it over her shoulder by the tail, crushed head and long, forked tongue dripping warm blood down the back of her dress, leaving a trail of blood behind her. A black haze of bush flies and an exhausted group of kids followed the old women; we'd be filthy dirty and hungry again, chattering about getting a big fire going for the feast of goanna and bush tucker. As we passed our house on the way to the Aboriginal camp, we would ask Mum if we could go along to the camp to eat. She always allowed us to go and one of the camp people would walk us home in the dark after dinner.

These hunting trips occurred at least once a week. At all times we were prepared with our hunting equipment, so that we could leave at the call of the old ladies. The men never went hunting with the women and children; they went their separate ways, making boomerangs, didgeridoos and spears, and chasing bush turkeys and kangaroo for food.

⟶

Once, when I was about eight or nine years old, an argument brewed between Bill Tapp, Banjo and Georgie when some of their extended family had come to live in the camp. Two of the young boys were working in the cattle yards. The cattle were wild and dangerous, it was the end of a long, hot day, and tempers were prickly. Bill Tapp yelled at one of the young boys and poked him with the drafting stick, telling him to hurry up or 'they would all get killed'.

The Aboriginal men took offence and decided to pay Bill Tapp back. After lunch break, the men came into the cattle yards and as Bill Tapp turned away from giving them some orders, one of the men lunged at him, stabbing him three times in the back with a castrating knife. A German man called Horst and young Ivan Woods jumped in and broke the fight up.

Bill Tapp was taken back to our camp, where Mum dressed the heavily bleeding stab wounds. After some intense discussion, they decided they needed to confront the issue immediately to stop things erupting into a major fight: the Aboriginal people outnumbered our family.

They went up to the Aboriginal camp, Mum with shovel in hand, Horst with a big stick and Bill Tapp with the Luger pistol in its holster on his belt. The people at the camp were very agitated and the situation very tense. Banjo, Georgie and some of the other men were carrying boomerangs, and the women, Daisy and Dora, were carrying nulla-nullas.

The rest of the white people were lying low, peeking from behind yard posts and buildings, trying to hear every word, fearful of the outcome. This was a terrible confrontation between two groups of people from vastly different cultures and deep language barriers. Everyone was scared of how far things would go.

Bill Tapp was not the traditional standover boss or an overly aggressive man, but on that day he had to establish leadership and authority for the future running of the property, to keep the community living and working in harmony and all the people on the station safe. If Bill Tapp was not able to do this now, then he would lose the respect of the employees, which would be disastrous.

There were some angry exchanges and pacing back and forth, and shaking of nulla-nullas and boomerangs in the air, but somehow Bill Tapp was able to talk to them and calm everyone down. The argument was defused and it was agreed that everyone would go back to work the next day.

My mother said that it was a very tense twenty-four hours. She said, 'I don't think I would have used the shovel, but it was the first thing that came to hand, about the only thing I could use as a weapon if needed.'

Banjo and Dora remained loyal employees for fourteen years before moving back to their country, Daguragu. The Wave Hill Walk Off of August 1966, when Aboriginal workers walked off the job on Vesteys' cattle station in the Territory, paved the way for their return to their country. The walk-off was a result of a strike and stand-off by the Gurindji people, led by Vincent Lingiari, demanding that the British Lord Vestey, who owned Wave Hill Station, pay wages and provide living conditions equal to those of the white stockmen. At this time the Aboriginal stockmen were paid in tobacco, tea, sugar, flour, blankets and basic clothing. Vincent Lingiari led the walk-off of 200 Aboriginal stockmen, house servants, and their families from Wave Hill. The strike attracted national media attention and the support of the unions. The Gurindji walked off Wave Hill Station to Wattie Creek, whose Aboriginal name is Daguragu, about 30 kilometres to the west, where they set up camp. After a strike that lasted seven years, they won the battle and were awarded equal pay conditions. In 1975, Gough Whitlam's Labor government negotiated with Vesteys to give the Gurindji back a portion of their land, and the handover was made on 16 August 1975 at the community of Kalkaringi, 8 kilometres away from Daguragu

Aboriginal people were included in the NT Cattle Industry Pastoral Award in 1968.

The walk-off had a profound effect on the cattle stations, including ours. Our founding Muttburra/Gurindji family of Banjo, Daisy, Dora and Georgie all returned to Daguragu in the early 1970s. Dora passed away not long after their return.

The social fabric and payment of Indigenous workers during that time included not only keeping the workers but also their large extended families who were housed and provided with basic stores. When the equal pay structure became law it meant that the pastoralists couldn't afford to keep the extended family of women and children in food and clothing, schooling and healthcare. At Killarney we provided a home for up to thirty women and children related to the stockmen who worked there.

It was time for change and a fair deal for the first people of our country who were treated abysmally by many pastoralists and Australia in general.

I felt sadness for the loss of the wonderful people who treated me like their own, who had been so integral to my youth and to who I am now.

Over the years I would hear news of the family. Banjo was murdered by a relative in a family dispute. Georgie lived a happy life at Kalkaringi and Daisy also lived a long life, and both passed away in their home country.

I now work with the people of Kalkaringi and Daguragu through my position at the Victoria Daly Regional Council and drive out there, 500 kilometres west of Katherine, about every eight weeks. I have reconnected with many descendants of the people I knew in my youth, including Daisy's daughters Kitty and Violet, both old and frail but still full of stories about the early days. They speak of their love and respect for my parents and in particular Mum, because 'she bin give us clothes and bin look after them kids good way.'

I have reconnected with Old Jimmy Wavehill and his wife, Biddy, well into their seventies now, who were a young couple who walked with the people from Wave Hill to Wattie Creek in 1966. Jimmy has been active in the development of Kalkaringi, a much-respected elder who still wears his stockman outfit of a long-sleeved shirt, jeans, RM Williams boots and Akubra hat every day.

Chapter 5

MAYVALE BORE

WHEN MY MOTHER MOVED TO KILLARNEY WITH BILL
Tapp she was still technically married to Terry Clements,
my biological father. It was Bill Tapp's mother, Sarah, who
found a lawyer who could finalise my parents' divorce,
as neither of them could afford such a thing. Sarah Tapp
had a pressing reason, too: Mum was pregnant with Bill
Tapp's first child, and her fourth.

The divorce was finalised in time for Mum and Bill
Tapp to marry in August 1962, three weeks before my
brother Sam was born.

The living conditions on Killarney were hardly kind to
the mother of a newborn, let alone one who already had

three children to deal with. For one thing, the little black bush flies were relentless. They clung to the corners of our eyes and mouths to suck out every skerrick of moisture. They covered our backs in a dark mass, like a swarming blanket. They bombarded our food and we had to lift them out of our pannikins of tea. They ate the soft flesh around the cattle's eyes. We kids also had constant bung eyes and boils. Moreover, there were always thousands of black ants in the food – but no one bothered about them, we just picked them out and kept on eating. Snakes, goannas, spiders, ants, lizards were regular visitors looking for warmth in our swags, along with the odd mad cow stamping through the camp fire, knocking over tables and drums of flour and ripping the tent cover, looking for water.

Mum was terrified of the snakes, and the cattle, and the dogs, and the horses – she never learnt to ride. There wasn't much on Killarney that didn't scare her. She would scream out, 'Bill, Bill, there's a snake in the swag!' as she scooped up the baby in her arms and backed away, trying to keep an eye on the unwelcome visitor. Each time there was a snake nearby, Billy and I loved to go into battle with a long stick, as Mum yelled, 'Get out of the way, you kids! Get out of the way!' Her cries did little to deter us. Probably we were a bit silly, because we didn't realise how dangerous those snakes could be. None of us ever got bitten, though, so maybe the long sticks did their job. The

2819 square kilometres of bush that was Killarney Station were my playground and I loved every inch of them. There was always something interesting around every corner, be it a fat, juicy bush turkey that ended up on the camp fire for dinner, brumbies and wild donkeys disappearing through the bush, or a little water hole where the snakes, goannas and kangaroos came to drink. But all of the station activities centred on the mustering of wild scrub cattle, building fences and yards. I loved mustering and I would hang around the cattle yards, trying to help but no doubt being a nuisance. Billy and I jumped on the back of a truck at every opportunity to go and kill a bullock for beef, or to check fences and bores.

In the very early days there were no cattle yards to hold the cattle, so everyone had to take it in turns to keep an eye on the herd to make sure they stayed where we wanted them to. Billy and I learnt to ride horses very early and loved to do the night watch. This involved riding our horses slowly around the cattle at night to keep them settled so they did not wander too far away. Everyone was allocated a two-hour watch, which they completed in pairs and then returned to camp to wake the next couple to take over. The first watch in the evening and the last watch at daylight were called the dogwatch. Everyone wanted either the first or the last watch so they could get a full night's sleep but there was a pecking order, with the older and more experienced stockmen getting these shifts and the young ones getting the shifts at midnight and the early morning hours.

I always felt safe when I was out on watch. I was doing something I loved – riding a horse and being out in nature – and I also felt responsible, like I was contributing something. Even though I was a child, it was important to me that I played a part in the bigger enterprise that was Killarney. I never had much sense that I was separate from the adults, because we all had our jobs to do.

While the night-watchers were on horseback, everyone else slept with one ear to the ground. If there was the slightest change in the mood of the cattle everyone would sit bolt upright, ready to leap onto the back of a horse. If there were dingoes nearby, the cattle would be restless and were likely to take fright and rush. The squawk of a night owl could be enough for the mob to lurch into a panic, stampeding blindly into the night. Both of these situations were to be avoided – not only could the cattle cause a lot of damage when they stampeded, they would also have to be mustered again, and that could take days.

When I was learning to ride, I was allowed to go on the first watch with either Banjo or Georgie while the rest of the camp were having dinner and settling for the night. Banjo would lead the way and I ambled along behind. He sang corroboree songs in a low monotone, over and over, for the whole of his shift. His soothing songs flowed across the thick dust into the sunset, willing the cattle to settle for the night. I didn't realise then, but I was privileged to attend what were essentially private concerts every night. Banjo's songs were a part of my childhood – part of my Dreaming – and therefore precious to me. The Aboriginal stockmen also told us stories about debil debils and the Kadaitcha Man, just as Old Dora and Daisy did, although the stockmen's stories always seemed a little more scary. I was terrified of one story of the dingo that was bigger than a man, with eyes like car headlights, which would take you away in the middle of the night if you were naughty. The dingo could carry you in his teeth across the plains and up to the caves, high into the hills. I kept my manners and my eyes peeled in case I ever saw this dingo. I am happy to say that I must have been a good girl, because I never did see it.

At this age, Billy and I did everything together: getting into trouble, riding horses, fighting. We were often in competition with each other; if we were on horseback we'd be competitive about who was the best rider and how fast we could gallop, and we liked to show off our skills to the stockmen. As a girl, I felt I had to prove myself a little bit more. Not that anything was said to me – it was just a feeling I had, that I had to always keep up with the boys. Within Aboriginal stockman society, women didn't really have much status. And while I wasn't brought up to believe that I was of lower status than my brothers – certainly not by my mother – I did feel quite competitive about wanting to be as good as the boys. And the expectations on me were that I should be good at everything, even though I was a girl and I was meant to be staying home and helping Mum. I wanted to do the same things that the blokes were doing, which was mustering and galloping around and learning to drive very young. But I didn't like changing tyres or killing snakes – I was happy to let the blokes do that!

Billy, by contrast, was comfortable with his abilities and who he was. The expectations of what he would do at that time of his life were very clear: if he was a good horseman, a good stockman, that meant he could do anything, he could fence, fix motors; being out in the stockyard was how he grew, it was just part of his apprenticeship.

Mum expected equality for all; she wanted her girls to have equality with men. So she didn't stop us – me, particularly, in the early years – going to the cattle yards and branding and drafting, mustering, driving, anything like that. And some of the things Billy and I got up to were outrageous. In retrospect, they were probably quite dangerous. No one would let their kids do those things now. But we learnt survival skills and hand–eye coordination, as well as an ability to move quickly that stood us in good stead for sporting activities. These were life skills that would prove to be very useful for all of us. And we all survived our childhoods, so we must have been doing something right.

While Billy and I were getting up to mischief, Shing was still too young to join us; instead, she got on with being a cute little blonde-haired girl with flies in the corners of her eyes and only a pair of knickers on, following the Aboriginal women around the camp. Everyone loved Shing. Bill Tapp used to call her 'my little Shingy' and he doted on her.

When I think back, I realise how lucky we were that we got a stepfather who loved us all. The way he accepted us – how he took us on as his own – was unusual. Bill Tapp was in love with Mum, but along with his passion for the station and his inner obsessions, there was no room for being a rollicking, cuddly father. As a spoilt only child himself, he did not have the parenting skills that one expected from fathers in the twentieth century, so Mum probably did her bit to make sure there were no problems between us and Bill Tapp – she wouldn't have let him think that he ever came second in importance to the kids. Fundamentally, though, I think he just loved Mum so much he took everything that came with her; he never really thought too hard about it. Us kids didn't think too hard about it, either – he loved our mum, so from the time we moved to Killarney he was our dad, and that was that. He was also the man who was responsible for the biggest adventure of our lives: Killarney. It was impossible not to love someone who could give us so much, so freely. Bill Tapp never begrudged us his home, nor was he stingy with his heart. He was, in every way, our father.

———

Despite the constraints of our existence, we lived happily for the first two years at Mayvale Bore, even though the water supply was thick, dark and murky, and the quality and quantity dropped to unsustainable levels. Soon, everyone suffered from constant dysentery. Given that we couldn't survive without water, it was time to move and for Bill Tapp to find a place to build a permanent homestead.

Bill Tapp decided that we must move a further 30 kilometres off the main road and into the centre of the property, to Gallagher's Bore, where the water quality and supply were better. It was also a more central location to work from and less barren than Mayvale Bore.

In 1963 we packed up our home, such as it was. Everything fitted on the back of a truck and was moved to the new location to await the construction of our new house. None of us was going to miss the bough shed – it might have been our shelter but in reality the whole of

Killarney was our home. Which was just as well, because we would live in a new bough shed while the homestead was being built. It didn't make much difference to me – it had been great fun sleeping in our swags, then we'd had the verandah of the shed, and now there was a new shed. Nana's house in Katherine was a distant memory and I don't recall ever regretting that I was sleeping under the stars instead of inside Nana's house. Probably I was glad to have more space: Nana's house had always been full to bursting, and on Killarney we had hundreds of kilometres to call our own.

The only existing resident at Gallagher's Bore was a little old white man called Bill Ardill, who was about seventy and had come from New South Wales originally. He was so grimy and dirty that his skin was brown and his white beard was stained yellow from tobacco. Bill lived in a broken-down shack that looked as if it would topple over at any minute. The shack was dark and hot, and we never went inside. Old Bill had a large outdoor fire where he cooked his food and made large slabs of thick, foamless soap, as well as an outdoor wooden table with a set of large butcher knives. He had eight ferocious blue heelers that followed him everywhere – another reason for us to stay away.

Every morning Old Bill ingested half a grain of strych-nine – granules of dingo poison, similar to rat poison – as an all-round medicine and vitamin pill. This was called a 'heart starter' and it was common practice among the old drovers and bushmen to self-medicate with this poison. Old Bill swore by the remedy. It must have worked for him, because he was incredibly healthy and strong. Other common bush remedies included oil of cloves for tooth-ache – this was a prized medicine – Bex powders, and rum, which was thought to remedy pretty much every-thing else. Old Bill also liked to boil up pots of green pig weed, which was apparently some sort of wild vegetable containing essential vitamins. He was very fit and alert, so we assumed that he knew what he was doing.

Old Bill spent all his time checking the water level on two bores and keeping the pumps going. He walked around the only paddock near the bore at that time, twelve square miles, every morning with his dogs. He was a well-spoken gentleman who had read widely and seemed to know everything about everything, particularly about plants and bush food. He kept almost entirely to himself and rarely interacted with the stockmen or Aboriginal people, although he visited my mother, who lived in her shed just 100 metres away, once a week to share a cup of tea and talk about world politics.

After Sam was born, Bill Tapp converted a shed 'up the flat' at Gallagher's, now called Killarney, for the family to move into, as another baby was already on the way.

This initial shed was a large room with a rusty brown corrugated-iron roof and four corrugated-iron walls, no door and dirt floors. We lived there for a short time, less than a year, but at last we now had some shelter from the rain and wind. The shed had a lumpy mattress on a board with four 5-gallon drums for legs for Mum and Bill Tapp to sleep in. There was a baby's cot and the rest of us, including Uncle Jimmy, Boko, Alfie Russell and Kenny Wesley, slept on the floor in swags. The men camped outside in the dry season. There was a table and a couple of rusted metal chairs and stacked boxes for storing clothing and as shelving. The toilet about 150 metres away was a 'long drop', a hole dug in the ground with a cut-off 44-gallon drum over it. The drum had a hole cut in the top. This amazing bit of engineering was surrounded by three tin walls and no roof, facing out into the bush. It was so hot you could not sit on the drum, so it had two wooden planks to crouch on. The smell was indescribable and the black haze of flies could be seen from miles away. The shed was quite close, only about 50 metres away from the mechanics' workshop where all the men camped; however, Bill Tapp was in the full swing of setting up his dream home now that he had identified the permanent position for the station. Nothing would stay the same for long.

My parents were playfully affectionate and loving towards each other. Perhaps as a consequence, Mum seemed to be constantly pregnant and, along with her own kids, there was the endless brood of dirty, snotty-nosed camp children, along with the Aboriginal mothers and the stockmen to feed and look after. It seemed in the early years that the only break Mum ever got from the station was to go to town to have the next baby.

As with everything, Mum came to terms with the wildlife. She'd never lived on a property before, let alone a station as rough as Killarney, but she adapted. Looking back now, I can only think that she loved Bill Tapp so much that it didn't occur to her *not* to adapt.

We also learnt about the cycles of life. Cattle were killed for us to eat, and they died for other reasons too. They perished in dams, and died whilst giving birth, from heat exhaustion, from TB or tick fever, or from being mauled by dingoes. Life and death were raw and exposed. This random and devastating aspect of life was brought more starkly to reality with human tragedy, when Boko drowned in the Katherine River during the wet season of March 1963, when he was just seventeen. He had gone to town to see Nana at a time when the Katherine River was in flood. He and his girlfriend were at the Low Level when she became caught in the undertow. Boko jumped into the flooding river to save her, but he hit his head on the weir. The whole town searched for him all night, but he was found a few hundred metres downriver the following morning by his brother Jim.

The message of Boko's death was delivered to my mother by the Salvation Army minister, Captain Victor Pedersen, who flew his little Tiger Moth plane out to Killarney for the purpose. It was too wet to land, so he flew low over the house a couple of times, waving a white rag to alert us that he had a message. He then dropped a note wrapped around a rock the size of a cricket ball. Bill Tapp had left on horseback with some of the Aboriginal men that morning, taking a pack donkey and swags to mend broken fences and muster some cattle on the way home, so Mum sent our mechanic, Pat Quirk, to deliver the news to him. The message that Mum's young brother had died in a drowning accident was also delivered over Radio VJY, so everyone in the district was aware of the tragic accident.

With the wet season well and truly set in, the road was too wet and boggy for Mum to get to town. She wasn't able to attend her youngest brother's funeral or be there to comfort her mother. It was another lesson for me in how much the seasons of the Territory affected our lives, for bad as well as good. The wet season could be as dangerous as the dry season, in very different ways. It wasn't the first time that the Wet had claimed a victim, or kept someone from attending something important. It wouldn't be the last, either. I would keep finding that out, year after year, on Killarney.

———

As we lived in the corrugated-iron shed Bill Tapp began to build onto another tin shed further away. It had three tiny rooms with no doors, little playhouse windows with tin louvres, a tin roof and a rammed-earth floor. Bill Tapp added fibro walls and another two rooms, a verandah and a cement slab floor. The food, saddles and pretty much everything else were stored in the rooms so they would not get wet. We all slept in one area, where the rain often swept in and soaked everyone and everything. There was no running water. In the wet season the water leaked through the nail holes in the roof and in the dry season the bitter winds and dust swirled through the creaking walls. Water was carted from the bore on the back of a truck in used 44-gallon drums and deposited along the wall near the kitchen. When it was needed for cooking, washing and having baths, the water was siphoned into buckets. There was a gutter on the shed roof that spilled water into some open-top drums in the wet season.

When I asked Mum about the early days on Killarney she said, 'Everything revolved around water in those first few years. Our first home was only a few hundred metres away from the bore. The shed had a few fibro walls, a kitchen, an old wood stove and 44-gallon drums full of water outside the back door. There was an outside bathroom that consisted of a shower, made from a tin bucket with holes in the bottom slung over a beam, three walls and no door, on a slab of cement. The wind whipped through the shower in the cold weather so we didn't use it too often. I bathed the kids in a bucket of warm water.

'On one of the many times that the bore broke down, we had to move perishing cattle. When the cattle got a smell of the water at the house, they would come charging, frantically trying to get to the water in the drums.

'At some stage, a big bull got into the shower, and he didn't know how to get out. It was pitch-black dark and there were cows outside, knocking over our precious drums, looking for water. I got the stock whip out to try to get rid of the bull. I had no idea how to crack it, but thought it might help if I swung it around my head and yelled. The bull was bellowing and blowing saliva and snot everywhere. The kids were all piled in the corner of the bedroom – that also had no door – wide eyed with fear. It seemed to take forever, but the bull eventually found its way out.

'On another occasion, Sammy, the pet donkey, got into the kitchen and ate all the loaves of freshly baked bread sitting on the bench, knocking over drums of flour, billy-cans of tea and bags of sugar. All the day's food was a big mish-mash mess on the stone floor. I was so furious. I chased him up the flat with a bush broom. But in the end I just had to clean it up and start all over again.'

The old rusty brown shed became the men's kitchen when we moved into the fibro house. We had a new 'long drop' toilet with three walls built for our private family use, about 100 metres from the fibro house and this one had a roof and a door that didn't close. Many a time we had encounters with king brown snakes, scorpions and great big redback spiders in that toilet. It was the scariest place on the station and a quick squat behind the wood heap – also home to snakes, spiders and lizards – was a much more attractive option.

Bill Tapp was a workaholic and perfectionist, and he expected everyone around him to be the same. The men who worked for him were given a Sunday morning off to do their washing and the only other breaks taken were to attend the Katherine Show or the Victoria River Downs Races. In return they were given an annual pay cheque and everything they needed to live while they were on Killarney. The conditions might sound harsh, but when you don't have to worry about where you're going to sleep or how you're going to eat, life is a lot less stressful. These men worked hard, for sure, but Bill Tapp also took his responsibilities towards them – towards all of us – seriously.

Bill Tapp's obsessive and kind nature became clear to all of us quite early on. He checked and double-checked that gates were closed and pumps and power points were turned off. He loathed cruelty to animals. Bill Tapp would not allow us to kill or hurt anything. This included insects, ants and flies. When the toilet clogged up with frogs he would make us take them down to the creek in a bucket to find a new home. Mum said that she knew the frogs and they all returned the next day.

If a bird was hit while out driving, Bill Tapp would lean out the car window and yell, 'Did any of you kids see that bird hit the bonnet? Do you think it died straightaway?' When this happened at night, we would snuggle down under the blankets in the back of the vehicle and pretend we were all fast asleep.

'Did any of you kids see that bird hit the bonnet? Do you think it died straightaway?' he would yell louder.

We would all reply, 'Yesssss, it's dead!'

But Bill Tapp would stop and methodically inspect the front grille of the car to see if the bird was wedged in there and possibly still alive. If there was no dead bird in the grille, he would set off. Another ten minutes down the road and he would ask again.

'Are you sure that you saw that bird? Was it killed properly?'

'Yessss,' the little voices shrilled through the darkness in our most convincing fashion, all the while trying to act very exhausted and tired and burrowing deeper into the swag. But we knew what was coming.

Bill Tapp pulled over on the side of the road. 'All right, you kids keep a look out on both sides and let me know if you see the bird.'

All the little kids would lean over the sides of the Toyota, cold wind whipping around us, looking for the remains of a wounded or dead bird.

'Do you think it was about here?' Bill Tapp would ask while we searched in vain for some bird feathers.

'Yesssss . . . it's dead,' we would call back, trying to get it over and done with as none of us had taken any notice where we were other than we were on the way to town.

'I think I'll just go a bit further, I think it was nearer to the Delamere turn-off, and if it's not there then it must be all right.'

We would continue to creep along the road, little heads peering out into the dark, looking for a dead bird. If Bill Tapp spotted a few feathers on the road, we would have to get off the back of the vehicle and search for a corpse. There was me, the eldest aged about nine and my younger brothers and sister aged down to about four years. We were all terrified of the dark and would scrabble around to see if there was an injured bird anywhere close by; however, we rarely found the creature and were relieved to be able to crawl onto the back of the vehicle and curl up under the blankets to resume our trip when Bill Tapp would finally turn the vehicle in the right direction, after much coaxing from Mum in the front seat.

My mother later told me he would continually ask her for clarification and reassurance. Did she see the bird? Should he turn back? Did she think it died instantly?

The radio telephone service replaced the two-way radio as the main source of communication in the late 1960s. One could only use the radio telephone for a maximum of twelve minutes and this conversation was interrupted every three minutes with a voice out of the ether. 'Three minutes, sir, are you extending?' the voice would say.

'Y-y-yyesss p-p-p-please,' Bill Tapp would reply.

He always went over the twelve minutes and drove the telephonists mad as he asked for further extensions. He told the women at the radio telephone exchange that he should have extra time because he stuttered.

No one was allowed to kill any animals for any reason other than if they were suffering or for food. We killed at least one beast a week for the meat supply. Despite the fact that the stockman, usually the head stockman Sandy Shaw, had been doing this for years, he would still get a half-hour lecture about how to kill the animal – Bill Tapp knew that animals had to die for us to be fed, but he also thought there was a right way to kill them.

'Make sure the cattle are settled,' he'd say. 'When you have picked out the killer, make sure it's right under you and that you have the gun ready and steady. Make a noise so when it looks up you can shoot it in the middle of the forehead.'

These instructions were given every single time, month after month, year after year. We kids went for most of the killers and though it sounds macabre now, it was a weekly outing for us, and we would always be questioned by Bill Tapp when we got home.

'Did Sandy kill that bullock with one shot?'

'Of course.' We would all nod our heads vigorously. 'Yes, he killed it with one good shot, right in the middle of the forehead.' Which of course he did!

Bill Tapp loved his animals and though he was very much a pacifist, I once saw him punch a stockman for hitting a horse over the head with a hammer. The stockman was swearing and jerking the horse around because it would not stand still to have its shoes fitted.

Bill Tapp said to the man, 'How would you like someone hitting you over the head every time you moved?'

The cattle, all 30 000 head of them, were treated with care and compassion. When mustering, Bill Tapp would make sure that all cows with new calves were left behind in the paddock so they were not rushed or trampled in the mob. He said we could get them next time around when they were older and stronger – he didn't want to stress the mothers or brand the calves when they were too little.

One of the favourite family stories that developed into the folklore surrounding Bill Tapp was about him stopping a mob of a thousand head of cattle and not letting them through a gate because there was a big track of ants furiously marching across the road. He placed some bread and syrup on the ground to make a track to divert the ants while the stockmen and the cattle waited patiently for him to signal that they could continue.

Most afternoons, Bill Tapp would go for a drive to check the stud horses and cattle in the paddocks close to home. As he drove he would question Mum.

'Did the chestnut mare look lame?'

'No, I don't think so,' she would reply.

'Are you sure she didn't have a bit of limp on the onside front foot?'

'No, I didn't notice.'

He would then lean out the window and ask us kids the same question.

'Noooo, she didn't look lame to me.' We knew what was coming next.

'Oh well, I'll just go back and check.'

He would turn the vehicle around and go back to double-check, making the horse trot by, while having a deep discussion with Mum as to whether the mare had a slight limp or not. If he could not be convinced, which was more often than not, he would write down the horse's brand number and description and send someone out on horseback to recheck the next day, and then the questions would start again: 'Did you get up close to have a look at that mare? Did you make her trot? Did she have any cuts on that leg? Do you think her foal is getting enough milk?'

In later years, all the vehicles had two-way radios, so no one could escape Bill Tapp's ever-watchful eye. He would radio in and ask that a bore be checked to see if it had enough fuel then radio back repeatedly to see if you were sure you had checked it properly. Did you close the gate, were there any cattle hanging around the trough? On and on it went.

Our family was well used to his obsessions. They were just the idiosyncrasies that families put up with, but it was very disconcerting for those who did not know him. They would get offended because he was always checking up on them.

Being the obsessive–compulsive that he was, Bill Tapp researched and planned everything to do with Killarney meticulously, from the buildings to the breed of cattle and the type of vehicle he would purchase. And he had planned this move to Gallagher's Bore with the same attention to detail.

His first job at the new station site was to build a large set of cattle yards. All the posts were hand cut, with the lancewood rails being transported from the Murranji Stock Route, approximately 80 kilometres away.

Whilst more fences were being built our new and final house was built in 1969 with grey cement bricks handmade on site. The bricks were a mix of grey cement powder and sand carted from the creek and pressed firmly into a metal mould that made six bricks at a time. We had a lot of fun making the bricks and seeing our new home grow. Bill Tapp had drawn a design by hand and given it to the builder, Bill David, from Katherine. The low-set house had a large kitchen and lounge room area. There was a big bedroom with an ensuite for Mum and Bill Tapp and an adjoining small room with no door for the baby of the day. There was a pantry-cum-store room and this was also where the medicines were kept. There was a massive big room divided by a built-in wardrobe, with two sets of double bunks in the main area for the boys and Shing and me on the other side in another set of double bunks. Out the back door from our room was a separate building about 50 metres away with an office, outside toilet, laundry and store room. The whole of the front of the building was covered by a large, sweeping verandah. All the carpentry in the house was done by Don Drury, a survivor of the Korean War who lived with us for many years as the new buildings were constructed. A school was built with one large classroom and a single bedroom and kitchenette for the teacher.

As soon as the brick house was habitable we moved from the fibro and tin shed into it even though it did not have any doors or windows. Our old shed was then utilised as the men's kitchen and sleeping quarters. One room was set aside for the cook to sleep in, the middle room was a pantry, and the third room was for the head stockman to sleep in. All the other employees camped along the back verandah on wire beds. The front verandah was set up as the dining room, open to the bitter winds of the dry season and whipping rain in the wet season. This served as the men's quarters until an eight-bedroom men's quarters was built in the early 1970s along with two 'married houses' – two-bedroom cottages for the white married employees such as a mechanic and head stockman. These were followed with a new 'men's kitchen', which was a large dining room on one end and a state-of-the-art kitchen with stainless-steel sinks, big gas ovens and industrial fridges in the middle, and a guest dining room on the other end.

Finally two single-bedroom motel units were built for the ever-growing number of visitors. There wasn't too much spare room in our house for extras.

In the early 1970s Bill Tapp decided to pull down the old wooden cattle yards he had built by hand and make new steel yards. They had to be the biggest and the best in the country.

Mum and Bill Tapp planned the layout of the station, including gardens, deciding to plant hundreds of *Ficus hilli* trees in straight rows along driveways and house fences, providing much-needed shade around the buildings and cattle yards. The trees spread octopus-like tentacles of roots that lifted cement floors and cracked walls in their burrowing to find water in the hard black soil. Mum did not like cooking and could not sew but she loved gardening and planted trees and flowers everywhere. She loved petunias and had them along the front of the house and school and in garden beds at the 'Recreation' area. The little coloured flowers flourished in planters made out of cut-off fuel drums and old tyres. There was a succession of alcoholic gardeners who mowed and weeded and invariably pulled out the new petunia seedlings or mowed over new shrubs just taking hold, but, despite this, the bougainvilleas exploded in their glorious reds, mauves and purples over gateways, fences and tank stands, and the poinciana trees along the front of the men's dining room caught on fire in a canopy of red in September.

—

Mum's fifth child, Joe, was born in December 1963; the sixth, Ben, in June 1965 and he was followed by William in July 1966 – that made a run of four boys in the middle of the family. I never felt pressured to help out with the babies each time a new one arrived, it was just part of life. I looked after the little ones around me, the ones who had grown out of babyhood, although I ended up doing a lot of bathing, changing nappies and making bottles anyway. I felt like I was doing my share.

I can't imagine that my brother Billy felt that he had to help with the other children, but I still didn't feel downtrodden by my role: I revelled in family life. I just loved the way we lived and all those kids being around, and even when they got a bit older and were little nuisances,

I loved them anyway. They were always there. Just part of life, like having a new pile of poddy calves to feed. There were lots of nappies and baby bottles around the house for so many years that it seemed normal. Our lives as kids weren't that much different to those of the adults around us. We were living in a very close community – it was only a couple of hundred metres from our shed to the men's quarters and a couple of hundred metres more to the stock yards. Everything was so close that people could watch out for us. All the kids, both black and white were just part of life on the station. We weren't excluded from anything, including the hard things. We didn't have a flash house where kids were sent off to the bedroom when the sun went down because adults wanted to talk. Certainly the first ten years of our lives were not like that at all. It was all in together, all the time, for every single person who worked there.

Chapter 6

A GROWING EMPIRE

BILL TAPP ALWAYS SEEMED TO BE WORKING FRANTICALLY, building houses, building new fences, putting in bores and building turkeys' nests, which were mud water holes created by pushing the dirt into mounds with a bulldozer to form a large above-ground dam. He hired the bore drillers Gorrie and Cole from Alice Springs, 1500 kilometres south, to search for a better water supply for the station and set up a number of bores and troughs. We observed the men from Gorrie and Cole practising the ancient methods of water divining, which involved making a T-shaped wand out of fencing wire and walking around with it pointed to the ground. When the wire detected a water table, it would quiver and pull towards the water and the drillers would set up in that area. Still, they spent a long time drilling and had a lot of trouble finding enough drinkable water in some areas.

The search for water was a never-ending struggle as Killarney was a dry block with no permanent water holes. The Coolibah and Battle creeks raged into the massive Victoria River system in the wet season and lay dusty and dry for months in the dry. The Mayvale Bore was only 10 kilometres off the Buchanan Highway but produced a meagre 150 gallons of water per hour. The Mayvale water was also limey and rank; it was barely enough to quench the thirst of the family, stockmen and horses, let alone a mob of perishing cattle. When Bill Tapp first moved to Killarney, therefore, the most urgent need was to find a stable water supply, followed by building paddocks to bring the feral cattle under control. With Killarney being 2819 square kilometres in area, we needed quite a few bores spread strategically across the run so that cattle could be moved back to the central station area for branding and trucking off to the meatworks. Having good bores made it easier to muster the cattle who had to come to the bore every day to drink.

Old Norman Jensen was another of the characters who spent time on Killarney. He lived in various locations around the station as he searched and drilled for the elusive underground water. He, like everyone at the time, lived frugally and in incredibly rough conditions, just a tarpaulin stretched between trees to shade his food and belongings. He camped out under the stars in his swag in the Dry and under a makeshift lean-to in the Wet.

In 1965, Norm was drilling for water with a mud puncher, which had gone down about 40 metres when he felt a soft sponginess and the drill rods dropped quickly. The pump ground through the earth's rock and when he pulled the rods to the surface they brought flesh and blood with them.

Norm, who had lived in the bush most of his life, said, 'I pulled up several kilograms of what appeared to be hide and flesh. It was definitely some sort of animal that had died a long time ago. There was a lot animal flesh and beautiful brown hair, like fur. I went to Mum Hawke's place at Top Springs [the closest roadhouse to Killarney] and sent a wire to Darwin. A policeman came out and took a couple of tobacco tins off me and sent it to Darwin.'

The material was sent to Adelaide for testing but a report from the Institute of Medical and Veterinary Science – reported in the *Sunday Territorian* – failed to shed any light on the mystery. It said that no recent human material was contained in the sample and no recognisable animal tissue was present. An examination of the hair-like material was also inconclusive but the report commented that 'the material resembled jute fibres'.

Norm decided to plug the bore and moved 100 metres away to drill another bore, which yielded a good water flow. The new location was appropriately named Monster Bore. Norm always believed that he had found a prehistoric animal that had been preserved during the Ice Age. Because of this no one liked to camp at Monster Bore when mustering in the area – everyone was superstitious about the place.

Unlike the famous Lasseter's lost gold reef in Central Australia – which two of my uncles set out on an expedition to find in the early 1970s – the mysterious Ice-Age animal of Monster Bore at Killarney Station has not attracted further attention from monster hunters, so we will never know what creature the fur and flesh belonged to.

Very little had been documented about the country and cattle in the Victoria River district when Bill Tapp bought Killarney in 1960, so no one was sure how many cattle were on the property, although the previous owners, Eric Izod and Ivor Hall, had estimated that there were approximately 5000 to 7000 head of wild cattle spread across the whole property. Bill Tapp's first small muster yielded almost 1400 head of cattle and three-quarters of them were clean-skins, unbranded and therefore unclaimed. All the clean-skin cattle automatically belonged to Killarney and this proved to be our good fortune – this number in the first core muster meant that it was most likely there were a lot more than the estimated 5000 head of unclaimed cattle. As the country had never been fully mustered no one really had any idea of what the numbers were so the estimates were made on general stocking numbers across properties in the region.

The cattle were feral, and the markets were a long way from Killarney. Branding was carried out on a bronco panel, made from thick curved tree branches, hand-cut into wooden posts and placed deep in the ground to provide a frame to pull the beast up against it and flip it over on its side for branding. Bill Tapp would rope the clean-skins around the head from the back of his horse and drag them to the panel. The rope was secured to the saddle. The Aboriginal stockmen worked the leg ropes, catching a front and back leg to pull the beast off balance and onto its side. As soon as the beast hit the ground, another man would pounce onto the horns to hold the head down. The Killarney ITH brand – from the names of Killarney's original owners, Eric Izod and Ivor Townshend Hall – was burnt onto every clean hide that came through the cattle yards and each beast was earmarked with the numeral 7.

Each cattle station had a different shape of earmark so that cattle could be easily identified from a distance. Branded cattle from neighbouring properties were returned to their owners. Most of the bulls were scrawny, tough and wild, so were castrated to grow into bullocks for the markets and the branded cows were sent back out to the paddocks to breed with breeding bulls selected by Bill Tapp.

Wild horses were rounded up and broken in for riding. Each person in the stock camp would be allocated four to six horses so they could be rotated each work day and if any were lame or hurt they could be left aside until they recovered. If you had fifteen stockmen this meant you had to have a camp of at least ninety horses as well as the pack donkeys. As the old horses were pensioned off, new ones had to be broken.

There were no horse yards and very few fences, so the horses were cared for by the horse tailor, who knew every horse intimately. He fed them and hobbled them out at night with a small chain attached to two leather straps buckled around the horse's front legs to slow it down and inhibit it from wandering too far from the camp. At night bells were placed around the horses' necks. The bells helped the horse tailor find the horses in the early morning for mustering. Mules were broken in and trained to carry pack saddles filled with food, water, swags, cooking gear and tools.

The community rose before sunrise while the cook stoked the fire up. The stockmen rolled out of their swags and prepared for another long, hot day in the saddle, packing up mules to carry water and food. The battle for survival for the cattle was as hard as it was for the people who lived out in the middle of nowhere trying to tame and bring the herd under control. During the dry season, cattle grew weak and got bogged and perished on the edge of dried-up water holes, their eyes picked out by the crows. The cattle were infested with ticks that sucked their blood and energy, and the bush flies scavenged around their eyes, eating the flesh away

There were generally about six big musters and six small musters a year, covering a strategic area of the station where the cattle gathered around water holes. The stock camp workers would head out to camp at one of the bores or water holes and work the cattle back into a purpose-built paddock over a period of two or three days. They would then walk the mob 20 or 30 kilometres back to the main cattle yards at the station to be sorted and branded. These musters could yield up to 1000 head of cattle at a time. With each round of mustering and branding, the herd that Killarney owned increased and they were sent off to the meatworks in Katherine.

Very early on Bill Tapp was clear about having to breed horses to suit the climate and the harsh conditions of the Territory. He bought a thoroughbred stallion called Basalt. Basalt was sired by a stallion called Star Kingdom and a dam (mother) called Boxilla. Basalt's blood lines came from superior imported breeds in Ireland and he was a great grandson of Hyperion, who ran in the 1935 Melbourne Cup.

Bill Tapp bought the stallion in 1962 to add height and longer legs and bring finer bone and finesse to the breeding stock of thick-set stock horses in the Territory. He raced the stallion once in Katherine, where he won his race, and on return to Killarney put him with a select group of mares. Basalt's time at Killarney was short: he came to a tragic end when he was bitten by a deadly king brown snake and died. He had sired a few foals and Bill Tapp kept the females for the foundation of his breeding stock until he bought another stallion. Following the death of Basalt, Bill Tapp continued to research the breeds and blood lines that he thought would best suit the Territory and eventually in 1969 settled on the quarter horse, an imported American horse that was bred for its cow sense, quiet personality and strong constitution in harsh conditions.

Elders GM opened its first office in the Northern Territory in Katherine in 1968 because of the amount of work traded by CW Tapp, Killarney Station. They saw the opportunities to do business with the booming cattle industry and became Bill Tapp's money tree as they financed a wide range of spending sprees for new buildings, bores and fencing, vehicles, stud cattle and horses, trucks, helicopters, as well as providing the supplies at the station store with food, tobacco and alcohol.

In 1969, Bill Tapp flew south to the King Ranch bull sale in Bowral, New South Wales, to purchase new blood lines for the cattle herd. He paid the Australian record price of $20 000 for an 18-month-old Santa Gertrudis Bull: King Ranch Oregon, who became the foundation of a herd of over 30 000 head of cattle.

At the same sale, he paid an Australian record price of $12 000 for a quarter horse stallion, Quarter Commando. Bill Tapp believed that a quarter horse was more suitable to the harsh Territory conditions than the predominantly thoroughbred blood lines. Quarter Commando was the foundation sire for the station horses and Killarney Station was to become the biggest privately owned quarter horse stud in the world at the time.

The arrival of King Ranch Oregon and Quarter Commando brought out the whole station to watch them being unloaded from the truck. Bill Tapp led the gleaming chestnut stallion around, pointing out his regal head with its white blaze down the centre, and his thick, muscular body made for the harsh Territory conditions.

King Ranch Oregon was just a baby at eighteen months of age, but was soon put to work in a paddock full of specially selected cows. Oregon died after a good twenty years of service and was buried in a big hole near the bough shed where he spent his last days, close to the water and where Bill Tapp could see him outside the kitchen window every day.

As more and more people came to Killarney, Bill Tapp's empire grew – and he had more and more responsibility. He had to make sure that everyone was looked after, if not luxuriously then adequately. All up there were about twenty-five people working on Killarney when I was young, although we started with just ten. This increased to about forty people in the early 1970s. New people were coming into our lives, people with the skills needed to build a cattle station from the ground up. Fencers and yard builders, bore drillers and people to fix and maintain the bores, saddlers to repair saddles and cooks to feed the growing population, most of them staying for ten or twenty years. As the cattle numbers grew we needed more paddocks and more stockmen, and we needed more expertise. More fences were built to contain the cattle and more houses built to accommodate the people. In the late 1960s the men built a large corrugated-iron workshop shed with a wood stove in a corner, and the single men lived there, camping outside on wire bed frames in the dry season and moving into the shed in the Wet. The shed was also used as a workshop to fix vehicles, storage and the station store. Generally, people got on pretty well – they were adept at living together, making allowances for a wide range of idiosyncrasies, cultural differences and altered mental states. People with obsessive–compulsive, bipolar or schizophrenic disorders, as well as alcoholics, seemed to be the norm; of course, we did not know those terms then. Generally, people were just 'mad'. A significant portion of the workers lived in the Aboriginal camp a kilometre away from our shed; the camp was always visible from our home because Killarney was so flat. A lot of the stories I heard when I was young were from the stockmen who would mostly talk about their droving trips – 'when I was a kid we drove 1000 kilometres with 1000 head of cattle' – and tales about their fights in a pub, their drinking feats or how their best horse had died. Storytelling was integral to our social gatherings. There was much that the Aboriginal people couldn't talk about, especially in mixed company, but they told stories about tracking lost people or tracking horses or finding a water hole. These stories fascinated me, and I learnt a lot about bush life.

One of the stockmen was Freddy Holtze, a brother-in-law to Nancy Holtze, who came to Killarney as a housekeeper at that time. Freddy was a happy, guitar-playing member of the Stolen Generation and graduate of the now notorious Retta Dixon home in Darwin, as was his mate Clifford Cummings. Freddy changed his name to his stage name of 'Brasso Jackson'. He loved to play country songs by Freddy Fender and Charley Pride and said he was going to save his money and go to Nashville, Tennessee. He instilled in me a love of country music and taught me how to play the guitar and sing Tammy Wynette, Skeeter Davis, Patsy Cline, and Dolly Parton songs.

Country and western legends Slim Dusty and Joy McKean were our idols and we knew every song word for word. We travelled to the Top Springs Road House one year to see Slim Dusty perform live. For us this was like seeing the Beatles, who had recently taken the world by storm. I first heard of the Beatles when my cousin Robyn came down from Darwin for the school holidays with a record. I fell instantly in love with Paul McCartney, as did millions of other girls across the world. My grandmother Lillian Tindill, who owned the frock shop in Katherine, sent Robyn and me a pair of white underpants with a black and white photo of the Beatles across the back for a Christmas present. I loved those knickers so much. How I wish I still had them!

One of our long-time employees, Ivan Woods, came to us as a fourteen-year-old from his large family in the Katherine region. He was just five years older than I was and worked as hard as any man. Others arrived on the station after being hunted out of town by the local police officer for drinking, fighting and hooning. Killarney was a haven and home – just as Bill Tapp wanted it to be – and most of the people who came for a season never left. Bill Tapp had created a place where they felt valued and safe – because they were. He was a good employer and while he might have been tough on his men, he had an empathy for them, and never took anyone for granted.

In the early days Mum operated a small store that opened once a week in a small, hot tin room at the end of the mechanical workshop, offering the most basic of essentials: matches and tinned tobacco, powdered milk, tea, flour, needles and cotton, sugar, salt, blankets, soap, razor blades, treacle, jam, tinned peas and golden syrup. The store was replenished every few months, depending on the weather and who was travelling in or out of Katherine and could pick up the orders. A big order had to be done in November to get us through the wet season because the roads were usually impassable until about May the following year. This order would include all the tinned food, tea, sugar, salt, flour and rolls of fencing wire, steel, fencing pickets, pliers, nuts and bolts, tin, cement, rolls of leather to repair saddles and make new bridles and halters. The stores were ordered over the crackly two-way radio, or by a handwritten order if someone was going to town. Everything was bought from the only two stores in town, Cox's Store and Katherine Stores. Sometimes Mum would order in fancy things such as hair oil, powder, hair pins and scented soaps, and pieces of cheap, colourful, cotton fabric, needles and cotton for the Aboriginal women to sew clothes.

Mum would open the station store for an hour or so once a week and the workers would line up to get their supplies. She would write their purchases in a book and deduct them from the wages that she wrote up in the blue leather-bound wages book at the end of the month. I loved helping Mum and looking at all the new shiny packets and tins of food lined up neatly on the shelves.

The Aboriginal residents were provided with a weekly box of stores that consisted of flour, baking powder, salt, sugar, tins of jam and treacle, washing soap and tobacco. Clothing, bedding and all personal items such as soap, shampoo and medicines were ordered from Katherine as needed.

These were the times before Aboriginal people were able to legally drink or buy alcohol, when clap sticks and didgeridoos played through the night at the camp. This was also the time of segregation, pre-1967 when Aboriginal people were given the vote, when it was against the law for a white person to cohabit with or marry an Aboriginal person. Traditional marriages were recognised for particular purposes by a Commonwealth Act and a number of Northern Territory Acts; however, Aboriginal people were unable to legally marry white people. Consequently, the result was the Stolen Generation, a law that forcibly removed children of mixed blood from their predominantly Aboriginal mothers and placed them into orphanages and church-run institutions.

The Aboriginal people had a keen sense of humour and would joke and laugh among themselves. It was a sense of humour that most people would not understand until you got to know them well. They loved to send each other up and would laugh at one another's mishaps and blunders, such as being a bit too slow to get out of the way of a cow, or falling off a horse.

They kept their strict family protocols in rapidly changing times; however, people had begun having babies outside of the skin system, which had existed for an untold amount of time and for a good reason. While there was a general disapproval of this behaviour, everyone was accepted into the big station family network and the little misdemeanours and inappropriate liaisons overlooked.

Tensions did rise to the surface at times as people from different cultures and different countries lived in Killarney's small community. There was an incident when Banjo, Georgie and another Aboriginal man named Martin protested about having to do 'women's work': Bill Tapp had made them cart water up to their women in the Aboriginal camp in buckets. In protest, the men put on dresses and tied red hankies around their heads and carried the water, two buckets full, slung on the end of a stick across their shoulders, just as the women did. While it was considered a bit of a joke, it was also a serious statement that these men did not do women's work and the women should, and would, carry the water themselves. The men were not asked to carry buckets of water in the same fashion as the women again – they could deliver the water on the back of a vehicle in drums instead. This was different, and acceptable, because the men could drive, and driving was not considered a woman's job.

I once asked my mother, who had adjusted to bush life quickly, how she felt about living with traditional people who spoke little English. She said, 'I was never lonely. I was quite surprised to find this sense of humour in Aboriginal people because, like most white people, I treated them seriously. As I got to know them I saw them as ordinary people, just surviving, living and laughing like everyone else. They laughed at all the right things – or at least the things that I found amusing, which is a little bit of a putdown of other people, or finding other people's pretensions amusing. They were very perceptive about white people's self-importance and could mimic them very quickly. Just a couple of words would get everyone laughing hysterically. Old Dora in particular was very perceptive, whereas Old Daisy was more the gentle giant.'

During the first years at Killarney, the Aboriginal Affairs department paid pastoralists forty cents a week welfare payment as compensation to the pastoralist to support an adult Aboriginal woman and her child. It was the expectation that the station provided everything to the large extended family of the Aboriginal stockmen. This included all food, clothing and housing. We were all living in third-world conditions and with little income that came in sporadically on the delivery of a truckload of bulls to the meatworks. My mother protested to the department and told the patrol officer: 'We are all living on the smell of an oily rag – how are we expected to maintain an adult person on forty cents a week? It costs forty cents for a cup of coffee in town.'

Mum was a great mentor to the Aboriginal women, trying to lift their health standards and get the kids to school. She wanted everyone to achieve in life and never held anyone back, whether they were her own kids or other people in the camp. We were all in it together, after all.

We all, black and white, lived in the same harsh conditions with poor housing and sanitation, water shortages, and lack of decent food, while working long hours in extreme weather conditions. We were also working towards a common goal: making life easier for everyone who lived at Killarney.

Bill Tapp respected Aboriginal people but he did not really relax with them. He was much more worried about social conventions and expectations. He was 'The Boss' and he was always mindful of that in everything he did. His responsibility set him apart, and it kept him apart in many ways. The responsibility would slowly start to eat away at him, too, because he had no one to share it with once it became a burden.

Chapter 7

RAINING FISH

THE NORTHERN TERRITORY HAS ONLY TWO SEASONS: THE Wet and the Dry – according to white people, anyway. It is easy to see why this is so: the variance between the two is dynamic. In the Wet, one can expect torrential rain, flooding rivers, 40-degree heat in the shade and what seems like a million flies and mosquitoes. In the Dry, the temperature can drop to minus overnight, the cold biting into your bones and sucking every bit of moisture out of your body; the blue skies are cloudless and the horizon endless.

Aboriginal people live by six seasons. They feel the subtle changes in the temperatures; they watch the receding water levels in the billabongs, take note of which animals are around to hunt and what berries, nuts and bush medicines are available. The seasons and the landscape are not only fundamental to the Aboriginal people and their spiritual stories, they are also fundamental to the day-to-day survival of people carving out a living in the bush.

For us there were the two distinct seasons out on the plains of the Victoria River Downs. Temperatures ranged from 50 degrees in the shade during the wet season and a million bush flies, to the dry season of bitterly cold winds that blow in off the Tanami Desert, when our hair would end up like straw and we'd have parched faces, cracked lips and two million flies all trying to live on us or in our food.

The period immediately before the wet season – always known as 'the build-up' – takes on a life of its own. The momentum gathers as the big white clouds roll in, cluttering up the once endless blue sky, each day getting hotter, heavier and blacker. After a long dry season, the anticipation and expectation of rain built as we thrashed in our swags, sleepless, hot and sticky, and the mosquitoes bombarded our bare, damp skin. The build-up can turn the most affable people into monsters. When the bad-tempered cook started abusing everyone because his skin was cracking for the want of a good blow-out on a big bottle of rum, we would smile and say, 'He's going troppo', or, 'He has mango madness'. That's what the seasons could do to us, and he was not the only one to behave that way.

All conversation revolved around rain: would it be late, would it be early, would it be a long wet season or a short one? Everyone had a theory about the Wet. A short cold season meant a long wet season or vice versa; if it didn't rain before Christmas then we would get a cyclone in March. As the clouds got bigger and raced across the sky, we waited, and waited, and the bad tempers and bets increased. The seasons held us captive, if not hostage, and we had no choice but to live that way. We all understood that we were part of something so much bigger than any one individual or even our lively home: we might have our theories and our hopes about how the weather would behave, but it would always do whatever it wanted and we would obey.

Banjo was a 'rain man' and he carried small pieces of clear quartz rock tied up in a red-spotted bandana and used these to sing the rain; we also placed large pieces of quartz under dripping pipes and taps to encourage the rain. To 'sing something into existence' is a common Aboriginal concept passed down over generations. The song is often in the form of a chant and is associated with a material object such as a quartz stone, a bone, or strands of hair. I am sure Banjo's innate knowledge of the country and seasons contributed to his success rate of 'singing the rain' when the big storms came rolling in. I didn't question his ability to do this. There are things, phenomena, that just are.

The build-up was also when the mango trees bore their fruit. My nana would send us mangoes from Katherine, where the trees were plentiful and the fruit would rot on the ground if it wasn't eaten or sent to hungry mouths like ours. We feasted on so many mangoes that we always got mango sores, a burn around the mouth from the high, acidic, vitamin C content.

During the build-up, the ants scurried to build their red hills and the kangaroos waited on black soil plains, looking towards the sky. The cattle stayed close to the bores and drying dams, and the stockmen burnt little piles of dry manure in the cattle yards to create a thick smoke to keep the flies away from the horses' eyes. Little orange-striped hornets hung over the puddles, gathering mud to build their nests under the eaves, tables and chairs at the homestead. Green frogs would come out of nowhere, millions of them, singing loudly under the down pipes.

When the clouds finally burst, we would run out into the rain in our pants, screaming with joy while throwing the red mud at each other, smearing it all over our bodies and in our hair and dancing like the Indians we saw in Hollywood movies. The stockmen would throw their hats in the air and the old Aboriginal women would stand out in the rain, smiling and swaying.

Bill Tapp would stand on the verandah, dark clouds almost visibly lifting from his shoulders because he did not have to worry about cattle dying around the rapidly drying water holes, nor about bore pumps breaking down.

One wet season we headed out for a rain dance. We jumped, squealed and slid in the mud, throwing mud balls at each other. There were thousands of little silver fish, no more than an inch long, flapping all over the ground and we ran around picking them up by the handful. We raced home, fists and knickers full of fish.

'Muuuuum, it's raining fish, it's raining fish!'

'Stay outside, you kids,' she admonished us. 'Don't come in here covered in all that mud.'

Bill Tapp came to check out the commotion and found a mob of kids all lining up with hands full of fish. Before we knew it, everyone was out, looking at thousands of little silver fish flapping on the red ground and in mud puddles. In true Bill Tapp fashion, he wanted to save as many as possible – hating to see any animal harmed – and we had to pick up and save as many as we could and put them in the water tanks and the troughs.

The raining fish phenomenon occurred a number of times – to this day it is not an unusual occurrence in the Victoria River region. It seems that, through a quirk of nature, the fish hatchlings can be swept up in a wind squall over a river and dumped hundreds of kilometres away by the rain.

While the wet season was, to a certain degree, a time to take a break, there was also lots of work happening, mainly repairing equipment and making new bridles, hobbles and ropes, pulling down bore pumps and vehicles and rebuilding them. The days were not so frantic in the wet and we did get Sunday off.

Every year, after the first rains, Bill Tapp loaded all the Aboriginal residents onto the back of the truck to take them back to Wave Hill Station for their initiation ceremonies and to deliver young wives to their promised husbands. Billy and I loved to go on these trips. We rode on the back, sitting on the swags with Daisy and Dora, Banjo and Georgie, all their worldly goods wrapped in old dresses piled up high along with the newly made nulla-nullas, boomerangs and spears for ceremonies and trading, and to be given as presents to family.

Bill Tapp sat in the front, driving, but we preferred to be on the back, the wind blowing through our hair as Daisy and Dora chattered excitedly in language about going back to the country to see their families. It must have been thrilling for the old ladies, who only saw their extended families during the wet season gatherings. It was a time for them to talk to their daughters and meet their new grandchildren, nieces and nephews; a time to share stories and sort out family problems.

The road to Wave Hill was a precarious trip of over 250 kilometres of rocky ridges and steep creek beds. The truck was old and rattly, and if we weren't bogged in mud we were bogged in bull dust, or broken down with a leaky radiator or flat tyre. We would wait on the side of the road until someone came by to help or until the bush mechanics fixed the problem. I was good at carrying rocks and logs to stack under the tyres to help provide grip in the mud or dust. The old ladies would look for bush bananas, berries and wild honey.

On one of the wet season treks returning from Wave Hill in an empty truck, we got bogged to the axles and could not move. My cousin Robyn and I were about ten years old at that time and Billy was eight. After hours of trying to chock the truck up with logs and anthills, it sank deeper into the quagmire. There was only Bill Tapp with us three little kids, and we could not provide the muscle power needed to push us out.

It was unlikely that someone would come driving by anytime soon, so Bill Tapp decided we should walk back to a construction camp near the roadhouse at Top Springs to get help. Barefoot, wearing only shorts, we walked all afternoon, stopping at creeks to cool off and picking wild berries and sour paddy melons along the way. We finally arrived at the construction camp at sundown, starving and badly sunburnt. The camp was empty as the residents had gone to enjoy the company at Top Springs. We had walked through 20 kilometres of mud in the heat of the day and our feet were raw. Robyn was suffering from severe heat stroke and was running a temperature. Billy had large watery blisters all over his nose and shoulders. We made ourselves at home in an old silver caravan set up as a kitchen and ate tins of bully beef and baked beans before falling asleep in another caravan set up with beds.

We spent the night in the camp and the following morning walked another 5 kilometres into Top Springs to send a radio message home for someone to come and pick us up. The construction workers from the camp were happily propping up the bar and were sympathetic and bought us cold drinks and lollies and a few large stiff drinks for Bill Tapp.

On another of the wet season trips we got bogged yet again while returning from Victoria River Downs. We were caught on a black soil plain with very few trees and spear grass standing well over our heads about 20 kilometres from home, so Bill Tapp sent Banjo and Georgie to walk in to the station and bring back a truck to pull us out.

As the hours passed and we got hungrier and hungrier, Old Dora decided that we would have to eat the grasshoppers that were whizzing around in plague proportions. Billy and I thought it was great fun as we laughed and pounced on the fat green and brown insects. I felt no remorse as they were thrown, alive, into the leaping flames and turned with sticks. We crunched on the crisp little bodies with relish. The grasshoppers didn't taste so good, but those poor little insects served their purpose by providing a bit of protein, a few vitamins, and filling a very hungry hole. Though I have had the pleasure of eating goanna, wild turkey, buffalo, wild bulls, lizards and a variety of birds, I have been ever thankful that grasshoppers are not a culinary delight I have had to partake in again.

Bill Tapp did not join us in this culinary excursion but waited patiently, periodically walking up to the truck and kicking a few tyres or wandering out to collect more logs and rocks to chock under the bogged vehicle.

It was never long before the wet season came to an abrupt end and we would be storing water in 44-gallon drums and drinking water taken from tin tanks, cattle troughs and muddy billabongs again. We still managed to break down regularly in the dry season as the old truck overheated.

All the roads in the bush were bad and caused much damage to vehicles so that walking – or 'Foot Falcon' as we called it – was a common form of transport, as was getting about on horseback. Very few employees owned cars and most relied on the station for transport. It was not uncommon for people to walk from station to station during the wet season when there was plenty of water around, but you needed to have your wits about you and a means, such as a gun and matches, of catching and cooking some food along the way.

Sadly, but not surprisingly, one such walking incident turned to tragedy in the 1970s when one of the employees, Jessie James, an older man who worked as a handyman and was a bit of a loner, decided to spend his hard-earned holiday pay on an alcoholic bender at the Top Springs Wayside Inn. This was not an uncommon practice for many of these men who had left their history and their families down south and come north to live in isolation. Jessie ran up a tab for accommodation and alcohol and when the cheque ran out he decided to walk the 40 kilometres back to Killarney. The people at the pub didn't notice he was gone and once they did, they assumed he'd got a lift with someone. No one at the station expected him to be returning home, so no one was quite sure when, or how, he left Top Springs.

The remains of his body were found a few weeks after his absence was noted, scattered along the side of the highway.

There were no transport or freight services so food, medical essentials and mail were picked up when a truck was sent to town. Shopping trips were always put off until the last moment, such as when food supplies were getting dangerously low or vital parts were needed for bores and vehicles.

One mid-1960s wet season we were going on a rare trip to Katherine for some Christmas shopping, only to be again caught on Battle Creek, a notorious creek crossing on Killarney about 30 kilometres from the homestead. The truck lost traction going up a steep riverbank and kept slipping back into the river, which was running about halfway up the tyres. Mum, who was pregnant again and could not swim, was pulling us off the back of the truck onto the bank as the truck slipped further towards the river before gently settling in the water.

As the sun was setting, it was clear we weren't going anywhere that day. Bill Tapp set up a tarpaulin strung off a tree on the side of the road and Mum settled for the evening with a couple of pillows and a blanket with her gaggle of tired, sunburnt and hungry kids crawling all over her. As the dank, dark wet-season night settled in, we tried to sleep under the little tarp in the pouring rain while being bombarded by mosquitoes as big as birds. It was a long restless night of babies crying and trying to get comfortable on the hard ground.

The truck was finally leveraged out of the river in the clear light of day and we headed off to town. But just a kilometre or so short of the main road, we not only got bogged again but the battery on the truck died. No amount of digging or cranking the engine was going to help this situation.

Bill Tapp sent a very faint message through Radio VJY to ask them to contact Killarney and tell someone to bring a tractor, battery and jumper leads out to us. After he sent the message he started to walk back home because the radio reception was so bad he could not be sure that the message had got through. He had walked about 15 kilometres when he was finally met by a couple of the men on the tractor.

Mum waited patiently covered in the usual haze of black flies, under a little tree while we played cowboys and Indians with stick guns around the anthills. The survival kit Mum always carried came into its own: we subsisted on black tea and a tin of Sunshine Milk to mix with the dirty red-brown water from the creek and a few tins of spaghetti and baked beans and a packet of Sao biscuits. She hadn't anticipated that what would normally be about a six-hour drive was going to take over two days and nights to complete. Once we finally arrived, my nana's house

– with its warm showers, clean beds and food – was, by far, better than any Christmas present.

The Wet often had an impact on how we would spend our Christmas and we had to do a big store order for goods that would last at least three months because once the rains set in we could not leave the station. One year, a truck loaded with thousands of dollars' worth of these food stores and Christmas presents was swept off a bridge into a raging river a week before Christmas. On the way home from Katherine, the driver, Ivan Woods, became impatient waiting for the rushing water to drop low enough to drive across it. Ivan and his mate, deaf Kenny Wesley, waited, despondent and embarrassed, on the side of the road for hours, watching the swollen river gush over the top of the truck, until they were picked up by another traveller. The neighbours came in and winched the vehicle out of the river.

The groceries, tobacco, matches, Christmas cakes, fresh fruit and hams, Santa stockings and gifts, along with bags of sugar and flour, were all fish food at the bottom of the river. Anything that was retrievable, such as tinned food, was saved and sent on. More Christmas presents and perishables were ordered over the two-way radio and another vehicle sent to town to pick them up. Somehow Santa managed to find his way along the boggy roads and arrive in the early hours of Christmas morning.

Ivan and Kenny were not the most popular people on the station that Christmas, but at least the tinned food, beer and rum were saved. We laughed for years afterwards when Ivan told the story of how he and Kenny surfaced after crawling out of the sinking truck's windows, only for Kenny to immediately jump straight back into the raging river. When he didn't come up, Ivan went after him and hauled him out of the water. Kenny fought against him, yelling, 'I've got to get my rum, my rum, MY RUM!' He dived back into the river and managed to salvage the bottle of Beenleigh Rum that was hidden behind the car seat.

Despite the hard times, the wet season signalled a time of festivities and fun. No matter how wet or how many vehicles were broken down and how many roads we had to walk, Santa always made it to Killarney. The Santa sack got bigger and heavier with each passing year as our family continued to grow. Santa always managed to leave at least one brightly wrapped present under the scrawny tree branch propped in a flour drum wrapped in faded Christmas paper, with a dusty, broken-winged angel on the top. No matter how low the food stores got, Mum always came up with a rich Christmas cake with white icing and plastic holly on top, a big hot roast dinner, and pudding that concealed silver threepenny and sixpenny coins and was covered with creamy yellow custard.

Christmases were always shared with those who had nowhere to go over the wet season. The Aboriginal families joined in and my mother made sure that there were presents for everyone. The men got Brut aftershave and a packet of Peter Stuyvesant cigarettes. The women received perfumes and pretty costume jewellery. Old Micko the cook would recite 'My Brother Ben and I', perched up on a flour drum with his little pink towelling hat, white singlet, shorts and odd-coloured thongs, waving a 'white can' around. In the Territory, beers are white, red, green, yellow or blue cans (Carlton Draught, Melbourne Bitter, Victoria Bitter, Fourex and Fosters, respectively). The table was piled high with delicious food, and pannikins of rum and homemade cordial. Sitting on chairs made from tree stumps and empty upturned flour drums in the heat and rain, we sang Christmas carols and shared homemade presents.

On Boxing Day all the women and kids would go swimming down the creek while everyone else recovered from their hangovers.

The dry season brought its own dangers, most importantly the drying dams, water shortages, and the much-feared bushfires in the later part of the year. Most often, the fires were ignited by a lightning strike in the build-up to the wet season. Early on, a lot of the country was unfenced and fire control practices were unheard of. The first sign of a bushfire was a tendril of smoke that grew longer, wider and blacker on the horizon. As the intensity of the dry season built, the grass dried and temperatures soared, we remained alert and kept a keen eye on the horizon for smoke. At the first sign, someone would jump in a vehicle and drive out to spot and identify the location and work out how many people and cars were required to fight it. There was no GPS technology then.

While waiting for the spotter to get to the location and radio back, the station went into top gear, fuelling up Toyotas and the grader, loading and filling 44-gallon drums of water and hessian bags to fight the fires by hand. A convoy of vehicles would head out, with Bill Tapp giving orders over the two-way radio to go to different locations on the fire front. No one seemed to worry that kids were piled up on the back of the trucks, barefoot and wearing just a pair of shorts.

We would douse the hessian bags in water drums on the back of the ute and slap away at the flames while the grader roared along the front of the fire, mowing down flaming trees and leaping grass fires. We walked for miles, slapping at the flames roaring way above our heads, at times racing back to a vehicle and speeding off just metres in front of the leaping flames that we could not contain. We'd return home with no eyebrows or eyelashes and burnt feet.

The snakes, goannas and kangaroos fled from the fire and the hawks and crows circled overhead. We stayed out all day and night, returning to the station or a nearby bore to refuel and fill the water drums. I always wanted to be right in the action, bashing a branch with green leaves against the fire snaking along the ground.

It was exciting for us kids to be fighting to save our country alongside the men. Some of the fires we fought were ferocious and destroyed hundreds of kilometres of country, raging and then smouldering for weeks on end. As I got older, however, I decided that this was not really a great form of fun and I was not so keen to be jumping on the back of vehicles to confront raging bushfires. How no one was killed, I will never know. In later years, with better land-management practices, fences were built, fire breaks were cleared along the fence lines and the increasing cattle numbers meant the wild grasses were eaten down and there was less fuel for potential fires. There are still fires but the pastoral industry now understands the environment better and practises controlled burnings at the right time of year, so that the burn intensity and damage to the flora and fauna are not as severe as they were.

The terrain at Killarney is very flat and we could see the red dust trails or the headlights of vehicle hours before they got to the station. The lights, however, were not always as they seemed, and on a number of occasions we saw Min Min lights.

A Min Min light is a glowing disc of light that hovers just metres above the ground. It follows you, never gaining or losing the distance between you and it. I was alerted to this phenomenon by the stockmen who said they had seen Min Min lights when droving in Queensland or across the Barkly Tableland in the Northern Territory. These stories were not told with a fear factor but as a statement of fact. I did not question these stories as I gained much traditional wisdom through living so closely and in tune with the land and its people. I am not sure what the explanation for them is, but I am convinced that I saw a Min Min light at least two or three times. On a couple of occasions, we saw Min Min lights while travelling to or from the station on very clear, brisk nights. The light would stop when you stopped to open a gate and then maintain the same distance as the car moved along the road.

One of our favourite places to visit was Gallery Hill, so named because of the Aboriginal paintings in the rock overhang. We often took visiting family, friends and dignitaries to have a look at the paintings, which had probably been made during the wet season, because the good supply of bush tucker when the rains came would have allowed families to live there for a while.

The rock paintings depict two magnificent Lightning Brothers, each about 2 metres tall, surrounded by drawings of kangaroos and goannas. The Lightning Brothers, spirits of the Wardaman people, are depicted in their full ceremonial headdresses, painted in red and white striped ochre. In the cave, on a ledge just above head height near the paintings, there were also the bones of a small child lying on pieces of paperbark.

We never touched the paintings or the bones and I hope that they remain as pristine as when I was a little girl standing in that big red rock cave, in awe of the people who travelled the vast dry lands, leaving their stories as large works of art.

In the dry season we worked seven days a week, taking advantage of the cooler weather. The stock camp were given a morning off after a big muster to catch up with washing and sleep, but it was back to work in the afternoon. We slept huddled in our swags on freezing dry season nights, watching the Milky Way slide across the horizon with its magnificent sparkling light show and shooting stars, the moon resplendent in her silver gown before slowly taking it off for a black, moonless night. The sky above was our own private movie theatre. The Aboriginal people showed us the kangaroos and dingoes walking across the sky and told us the Seven Sisters were bunched together waiting for their husbands. We marvelled every day at the rising of the Morning Star and the Evening Star, and at watching Mars, Jupiter and Uranus glide across the universe along with the man-made satellites steadily looking down on us.

The Americans put a man on the moon in 1969 but it felt like we were still living in the nineteenth century, thanks to isolation, distance, bad roads and the lack of modern communications. As they say, ignorance is bliss and this was certainly true for me, because we lived such a wondrous life in our own space and time, fully encompassed by the land, the traditions, the folklore and the seasons that we were part of and that were part of us.

It was a simple life in so many ways but I can't imagine having had a richer childhood anywhere in the world. Everything I needed to know about life – good and bad – was on that station. The cycles of nature dictated the cycles of our daily lives and how the business went. Just as the weather changed, so did the way we all interacted with each other. We could have a successful year when everything was going right or we might have a bad year when Bill Tapp worried about how he was going to take care of everything and everyone.

Just like the storms that rolled in and rolled on, though, it was all temporary and I grew up learning to manage the change.

Chapter 8

KIDS' GAMES

MY FIRST BEST FRIEND WAS OLD DORA'S DAUGHTER NITA. She was the youngest of the ten children in her family and I was destined to be the eldest of ten in my family.

Nita was tall for her age, skeletal thin, with a head of thick, curly black hair. The three middle fingers on her left hand were missing so the hand looked like a claw with just a thumb and little finger. This was a birth defect that didn't have any adverse effect on her ability to climb trees, make fire, dig for bush potatoes and kill goannas, just as all Aboriginal girls did every day.

We spent most of our time going hunting with Dora, whom we both called Mum. Nita was a couple of years

Me, aged about 18 months.

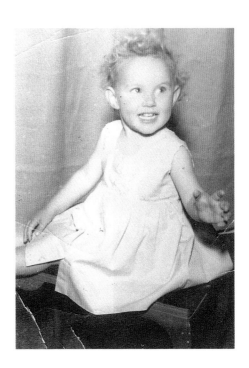

Billy, me and Shing with Mum, 1962.

At Comet Bore. Billy, me, Mum with Joe, Shing and Sam behind her. Our cousin Robyn Forscutt is sitting on the drum.

Young stockmen at the yards. Left to right: Joe, Ben, unidentified, Sam, unidentified, unidentified, William.

Bathtime at Killarney, c. 1964. Dora sitting in the tin tub; Nita with Shing in front; Daisy holding Joe; unidentified; Sam. The other Aboriginal woman is Bernadette: other children unidentified.

Christmas at Killarney, 1962/63. Left to right: Bill Hart, Norman Jensen, Bill Tapp nursing Shing, Bill Ardill.

Bill Tapp and Mum on their wedding day, 2 August 1962.

Bill Tapp with his mother, Sarah, and baby Sam, 1963.

1963. The first place we lived in with four walls at Killarney, at Gallagher's Bore, the current location of the station.

Bill Tapp, kneeling in centre, surrounded by the 60 people who worked on Killarney, 1971. *(Photo 4589555 courtesy NLA/Michael Jensen)*

The stockmen's kitchen on Killarney, 1971. Mick Nugent, the cook, presiding over the bread. Left to right: Shing, Ronnie Blitner, Kempe, unidentified, Jackie Farrell, Micko, unidentified. *(Photo 4589554 courtesy NLA/Michael Jensen)*

Happier times. Bill and June Tapp, 1973.

1971. The Tapp family with Bill Tapp's mother, Sarah – we called her Gram. Back: Gram holding Caroline, Toni, Billy, Bill Tapp; middle: Shing holding Daniel, Joe in purple shirt; front: Ben, Sam and William. Kate, born in 1973, is not in the photo.

Bill and June Tapp on Killarney, 1971. *(Photo 4588589 courtesy NLA/ Joe Brian)*

Shaun and me on our wedding day, Killarney, 15 May 1976. The bagpiper is Chris Atkinson.

Me on Bambino, early 1990s at Borroloola Rodeo.

older than me and was approaching puberty, and it would soon be time for her to be handed over to her promised husband – this happened to Aboriginal girls once they developed breasts and had their first period. The timing, therefore, wasn't fixed, but Nita and I both knew it was coming. Dora guarded Nita jealously from the greedy eyes of the young men in the camp and she would give them a screaming tongue lashing at the slightest sideways glance. She didn't want Nita's attention going anywhere else, nor did she want any other man making a play for her daughter before Nita came of age.

One day, Old Dora got wind that one of the older white men on the station had made advances towards Nita. She went into a fury. She started screaming abuse from the camp about a kilometre away, limping and swinging a nulla-nulla above her head. Between the yelling she would sing a type of chorus, a curse on the man. Every so often she would stop and pull off a dress and fling it onto the ground behind her, then start up the abuse again. She did this about four times, each time revealing another dress, until she came to a standstill at the front of the mechanics' workshop in her red floral petticoat. Her large breasts were heaving and gleaming with sweat as she continued to curse him. Everyone on the station heard and watched in awe and terror of the little dynamo, limping along on her bag foot. She left no doubt in anyone's mind that her daughter was off limits. If she even heard a word against Nita, the perpetrator would reap the rewards of her abuse and get a good flogging if she came close enough. She would even 'kill 'em proper way'.

The mechanic hid behind the shed till the dust settled and kept well out of Nita and Dora's way from then on.

All of Dora's older daughters had been married off to their promised husbands. They lived on neighbouring cattle stations and had large extended families, as there were two or three wives to each husband. Nita was Dora's baby and she didn't want to lose her to a man before it was absolutely necessary. Yet it was also important to the family honour and skin system that Nita go to the man she had been promised to before she was born. At one stage old Vincent Lingiari – who became known around the country due to the Wave Hill Walk Off – turned up at Killarney to try to claim Nita. There was a big argument and a standoff for a day or so, then Vincent left, empty handed.

Nita, Billy and I played together all the time. We didn't have any formal schooling in these early days so we had plenty of time to get into mischief and make up games that suited both our cultures. We spent all our time running away from the debil debils while being attacked by the (imaginary) cowboys and Indians. We fought them with stick guns and galloped off on stick horses and lay flat on the ground behind a rock, and had shoot-outs with the baddies hiding behind trees and down gullies. We made shanghais: a forked piece of tree branch that had two slings made from rubber bands cut from old tyre tubes tied to the forks, and a small leather piece to hold a stone to shoot galahs that gathered at the water trough, so we could cook them on a fire. Nita taught us how to make fire by rubbing sticks together and we would roast birds and lizards for our dinner. We collected empty tobacco tins, crushed one edge of the tin in, made a hole in each side and tied the tins to our feet to make horse tracks. We had races, rolling on empty fuel drums across the dirt to see who could get the farthest without falling off. We would run on the rolling drum, the rocky ground sending it in different directions, our arms flailing for balance. The drum would gather speed and eventually we would fall heavily on to the hard, hot ground. It was a game that left us with many bruises and twisted ankles but these did not deter us from the thrill of the competition.

We were always up to something. One day Billy and Nita were playing with a box of matches and burnt down the old wooden saddle shed with a tin roof and a wind break wall made of dried branches. Everyone was yelling and running towards the fire with buckets of water to put it out. Billy and Nita fled down to the creek to hide for a while, because they thought they would get a big hiding, but the situation settled down and the shed was rebuilt without too much animosity.

On another day, Nita, Billy and I were returning from one of our many trips to the dry creek chasing goannas, looking for sugar-bag and playing games. We had to climb through a barbed-wire fence. Nita was agile and fleet and usually led the way. She bounded up over the barbed-wire fence, slipped and fell, catching her leg on the wire. She swung upside down on the fence with the ragged point of the steel picket stuck into the back of her bent knee. Billy and I leveraged her off the picket to reveal a large, flapping wound. Her blood spurted everywhere.

We didn't have anything to tie around the hole to stop the flow so we just slung one arm each over our shoulders and dragged Nita along the ground, all three of us bawling our eyes out. Sobbing for breath, we stopped under a tree to rest. Nita was crying in pain and Billy and I were crying in terror at the blood pouring from her leg and fear of getting into trouble for being so stupid and going down to the creek without adults.

When we arrived home, Old Dora was screaming in fright and gave us all a good dressing down while wrapping a long piece of dirty rag around Nita's wound. When everyone settled down we then went to see Mum, who cleaned the wound with Dettol and bandaged it up with some antiseptic ointment and a clean white cotton bandage.

Nita was incapacitated for a few days afterwards and limped around with a little homemade walking stick but it wasn't long before she was mobile again and we were looking for a new adventure.

We loved playing down the creek. In the dry season we climbed the trees and ran up and down the river bed, creating tracks and camps. Every afternoon in the wet season we walked to our favourite swimming spot, where we had made a large mud slide into the water on one bank, while on the other we created a firing range with a pile of rounded mud balls for fights. The old women sat up on the sand bank with a fire and billycan of tea simmering, cooking bush tucker and making little johnnycakes for lunch. They settled fights and arguments and periodically lunged into the water to save one of the smaller kids from drowning, growling at us for not being careful and looking after them.

We had very busy lives entertaining ourselves. We would spend days playing make-believe in the old cars at the dump, making car noises, crunching gears and doing skids around imaginary corners. We dressed imaginary wounds and broken legs and drove furiously to town to save someone's life. We would muster cattle into the yards, brand them and load them onto the trucks to take them to town to the meatworks, and go shopping to pick up the stores. We made old milk tins into stilts by piercing a hole in each side and attaching a long wire handle to lift the tins in unison with our feet. We made up songs and chattered constantly in Pidgin English.

We made a whole village out of old bits of tin and fencing wire tied to the side of a car or a tree and little paths and tracks between the houses. We found old wooden boxes and lined them with empty food packets and tins in the kitchen. We used hubcaps for a washing-up dish and jam tins for cups. Nita, Billy and I each had our own house and we made a little bush broom to rake and clean the dirt around the outside to define the front garden. We would take some beef and bread and a little billycan of water from home up to the playground. There we made a fire and invited each other to share meals and a pannikin of tea while we talked about how to build important things such as cattle yards and fences, and how to muster cattle.

We loved to go on the annual trip with the stockmen to cut new branches to cover the bough sheds. This ritual happened after the wet season to re-roof the bough sheds and the humpies that the Aboriginal people lived in. One person would drive very slowly while others chopped the new fleshy branches from the young trees with an axe and throw them onto the back of the truck. We would run alongside helping, but the best part was when the truck was piled up to the roof and we would climb into the beautiful-smelling eucalypt branches and hide from each other.

On one of these trips, one of the Aboriginal men had chased down a big goanna and concussed it with a blow to the back of its head with the axe. The apparently life-less goanna was thrown onto the truck. We sat huddled under the branches beside the bloodied lizard, giggling and salivating about what a juicy feed Mr Goanna was going to be that night, when all of a sudden he came alive. Scratching and frenzied, he ran over the top of me and flew off the back of the moving truck onto the ground.

We scrambled and screamed and banged on the roof of the truck. It came to a screeching halt and we all fell out – in terror, in my case. The others took after the goanna to retrieve him for dinner, but he was too fast this time, despite the almost fatal knock to the head, and disappeared into the bush. We were hysterical with fright and laughter. The only proof that we hadn't imagined the whole thing was the small pool of blood that remained in the back of the truck.

The whole 2819 square kilometres of Killarney was home. Even though we had the homestead, we regularly camped in different locations, near water holes or bores, to trap, muster and brand the wild cattle. One of our favourite spots to camp was at Companion Springs. Companion

Springs was on the far western boundary, close to the Top Springs Road House, where we were able to buy lollies and cold drinks when driving past. Companion was a picturesque area with a series of cool water holes along the creek sheltered by large paperbark trees. We camped on the banks, a large tarpaulin strung between some large trees to serve as the kitchen and main living area. There was an open fireplace with a corrugated-iron fire break on the side of the prevailing winds. The fireplace had the mandatory billycans of tea, large tubs of corned beef and a hole for an in-ground oven, filled with hot rocks and coals.

We made Companion Springs our last muster for the year, as it was the last of the creeks that had water while we waited for the first rains. It was easy to trap cattle and horses at that time of year as they had to come in to water every day. There was a 'trap paddock', a fenced area around the water hole with a 'spear gate', made of wooden rails that were built in a V shape that allowed the cattle to squeeze through to enter the water hole, but they could not leave as the spear-headed end was narrow and had sharp ends preventing them from leaving.

Our camp was also located just a kilometre off the Buchanan Highway, the road that joined the Victoria Highway, travelled through Victoria River Downs and on to Timber Creek. The word 'highway' should be used with caution – it was a corrugated graded single-lane dirt road maintained by the Transport Department. However, this location also meant that we had a lot more regular visitors than we would get at the end of the 42-kilometre road into Killarney. Due to the massive area of the Victoria River Downs Station, there was an outstation called Moolooloo about 15 kilometres away from our camp, so we would get visits from the manager and stockmen.

Late one night one of the Moolooloo stockmen burst into our camp. The men were on a drinking spree at Moolooloo and others had decided to play a game with him. They had made him stand out on the flat and told him to dance while shots were fired from a revolver into the dirt, within centimetres of his feet. He danced in terror until he was able to make an escape with a bullet wound in his heel. He ran through the night to our camp, and was taken to Top Springs and then to hospital. These antics were often a test of a man's steel nerve and toughness and not really taken as a threat to life, so all was forgiven and once he had recovered he returned to his job.

On one occasion while camped at Companion Springs, Mum and Bill Tapp had gone for a drive to check the trap paddocks about 30 kilometres away and left us with Old Dora and Daisy. They had taken my baby brother Sam with them and left Billy and my three-year-old sister, Shing, who was regularly contained in a large meat-safe cot to save her from walking to the creek or into the fire.

Billy, Nita and I were playing around the fire making johnnycakes. Shing, who was skinny with a tangle of windblown, knotted blonde hair, was crying in the cot to get out. I lifted her out to keep her quiet and we continued to make our little johnnycakes, covering them in sticky golden syrup and eating them.

All of a sudden I heard a wrenching scream – Shing had stepped into the fire. I pulled her out, threw her on my hip and started running towards Daisy and Dora and the creek. Within minutes Shing's foot was covered in huge, ballooning blisters filled with fluid. She was screaming and I was terrified. Daisy took her and immediately started rubbing fat into the burn, which was the remedy at the time. Shing cried for hours and there was nothing we could do but wait for Mum and Bill Tapp to return. When they finally came home they took Shing to the Top Springs Road House to get treatment for the burns. Though my parents didn't blame me, I felt a terrible guilt for many years that it was my fault, because I took her out of the cot. Though the burns were quite severe and she had to be taken into Katherine Hospital, Shing soon recovered, and while she only vaguely remembers the incident, she still has the scars on her foot.

The old ladies always came with us and set up camp under trees not far from where our family camped when mustering. Mum allowed me to go to the camp at night and

I loved the smell of the fire and the bits of meat sizzling on the coals and the black tea. The women spent the days washing clothes in the creeks and looking after the kids. Long into the night they would sit on their swags, talking and laughing and singing. Dora, in her strong voice, and Daisy, in her high, sweet voice, would sing together for hours on end. These festive occasions tended to occur when we killed a cow for the weekly supply of beef, or when one of the boys had brought back a big bush turkey or goanna and there was plenty of meat to feast on.

Big logs would be thrown on the fire so that the flames were leaping into the night and the goanna – skin, guts and all – was tossed onto the bonfire. The skin sizzled, crackled and curled, and the women licked their lips in delight as they turned the big lizard backwards and forwards over the flames. When he was cooked, Mr Goanna was laid on some fresh leaves to cool before Daisy would pull out a huge butcher knife and slit the gut open, the cooked entrails spilling as she scooped out the kidney and liver to be eaten. She hacked off the tail and pulled the skin back, revealing the white meat and tearing off big chunks for us to share.

After the meal was eaten, it was time for other things: teaching Nita and me the women's dances.

'Come, you young ones, you gotta dance now,' Dora would say. 'You got to learn to dance proper way.'

She would do a demo for us, with her bag foot shuffling in the dust, breasts slapping and arms swinging in rhythm from side to side.

We would giggle and say, 'Noooo, we shame for doing that dance.'

Dora would continue to sing and sternly insist, 'No, you young girl, you come here, you got to learn to dance proper way.'

There were times when the Aboriginal people would receive messages of the death of a family member somewhere in the district. These messages were often delivered through dreams or spirits or sometimes a member of the family had walked across the country to deliver the message. All the camp would go into full mourning. Dora and Daisy would wail long and loud, swaying bare breasted in their half-slips, hitting themselves on the head with a rock until blood ran down their faces. The men sang long into the night in time to clap sticks and the haunting sound of the didgeridoo. The men and women did not mix during these times and the men carried out their ceremonies and mourning in an area at least half-a-mile away from the women.

They sang of their sorrow and asked the spirits to take the dead person back to the country, to their creation.

They would dance and drag leaves along behind them to clear away the tracks of the dead person so that the bad spirits could not find them. The rest of the station people paid their respects by keeping their distance and allowing the mourners to return to work when they were ready.

This mourning would go on for days and days, and once it was over no one spoke that person's name again. Sometimes people would say that they saw that person in their dreams or that the spirit had come back as a dingo or bush turkey, a goanna or a snake. I always accepted that this was real – it never seemed strange. It was what I'd grown up with, after all.

As I got older I learnt to ride and drive a vehicle but Nita was not allowed to go near any of the men, so she was unable to learn the things that I did. She had to stay at the camp with her mother, carting water and cooking and taking care of the old ladies. She could not speak to or have eye contact with her brothers. Though Dora guarded Nita jealously, she also prepared her daughter to go to her promised husband at Montejinni Station by teaching her the dances and stories and the family spiritual songs to support her when she left.

I didn't understand then that there was a clear time when Nita would go away, but one wet season she went on the ceremonial holidays and never returned. She took up her position as the third wife to Bill King Langandi at Montejinni. Her older sisters Mabel and Eileen were his first and second wives. I had lost my best friend and that was that – there was absolutely nothing anyone could do about it. Nita's fate had been set by ancient traditions before she was even born.

It was to be thirty-five years before I would see Nita again, very drunk in the main street of Katherine. I knew it was her immediately by her voice and the three missing fingers on her left hand. She was drunkenly arguing with her man and, just as her mother had done all those years ago, was throwing her clothes off to take him on in a fight. I calmed her down and put her clothes back on and never saw her again.

I heard a few years later that she was living in the long grass in Darwin and was hit by a car on one of the main roads as she staggered across the road late one night. I don't know if she was ever claimed by her family and returned home. Because of Aboriginal custom not to talk about the dead and call them by their names, I am unable to ask these questions.

Chapter 9

THE CATTLE YARDS

THE CATTLE YARDS WERE CENTRAL TO OUR EXISTENCE on the station. They were our school and our playground, where we learnt not only about cattle and horses but also about people, respect and hard work.

I loved the smell of the yards, the thick soupy dust and fresh, warm cow dung. I loved the smell of the burning hair that filled our nostrils when the branding iron singed its letters into the cowhides. I loved the sounds of the cattle shuffling and snuffling at night, the cows calling in low voices for their babies.

The cattle yard was where we were given our first horse to ride, where our saddles were neatly lined up on a long wooden rail, bridle and saddlecloth thrown over them to keep the sun off. It was where the saddler worked, threading long curved needles with waxed string, cutting strips of leather into hobble straps, stitching bridles, making new stirrup leathers with carefully measured holes for the buckles. The horse tailor brought the horses to the cattle yard every day and tended to their care, painting their sore backs with purple iodine and smearing their eyes with black tar to keep the swarming flies away. The horses would stand patiently, waiting for their iron shoes to be heated on the red-hot coals and shaped on the anvil.

The cattle yard was also where the horse-breaker broke in the new colts every wet season. Each horse hurled himself against the rails in confusion, eyes wild as the breaker threw the rope around his neck, talking, soothing and patting him to quieten down. The stockmen would buck out the newly broken colt as the onlookers yelled and cooeed, the rider hanging on for dear life to avoid being speared into the thick bull dust.

The cattle yard was where you had to wear the right uniform: blue jeans, Cuban-heeled RM Williams boots, a leather belt carved with your name and fastened by a shiny horseshoe buckle, long-sleeved blue shirt and an Akubra hat. None of that fancy Yankee stuff like in the movies.

The cattle yard was no place for wimps, tears or tantrums. It was where you were teased mercilessly for opening the gate too soon or too late; where you were labelled a sook if you cried for being slammed into the gate; where everyone howled with laughter if you were trampled into the dirt by a crazy cow.

In the yard, the young bulls were run into the long wooden crush, castrated and earmarked, then had their horns blunted with a saw. The stockmen rode the bulls out of the crush to practise their rodeo skills, the bulls jumping and twisting, horns swinging wildly, snot and blood flying as one of the other stockmen tormented them to make the bullock buck harder.

The stockmen liked to sit on the top rail for a smoko break, concentrating deeply as they slowly rolled the tobacco through their hands, cigarette paper hanging out of the corner of the mouth, eyes squinting through the dust. They bragged about throwing bulls, riding a buck jumper or the last drinking spree in town. They talked about their dreams, buying a new car, saving enough money to go south to see their mother, of getting a head stockman's job or buying a cattle station.

The government-employed stock inspectors were an extended part of the camp and spent days at a time on the station testing for pleuropneumonia, tuberculosis and tick fever, and applying bush vet surgery to help deliver calves, give injections and provide ointments and bandages for cuts and fly-bitten eyes. They tested for botulism and brucellosis and dipped the cattle for ticks.

The person who taught me so much about mustering and country was our head stockman, Sandy Shaw, who came to work for us sometime in the 1960s. He was a part-Aboriginal man whose white father had been a saddler travelling through the region repairing saddles on the stations in the 1930s. Sandy had a younger brother, Ringer Shaw, and they were both born at the neighbouring Victoria River Downs Station to their Aboriginal mother, Lily Anzac. Sandy was the eldest of the children and his mother went on to have many more children to her traditional husband.

Sandy existed across two worlds, living with his Aboriginal family when he was a little boy. Following his initiation and rites of passage according to tribal law at the age of about thirteen, he was sent to work in the stock camp. He was taught basic reading and writing while cattle droving with the white drovers who travelled the region delivering cattle to the meatworks and sale yards.

Sandy was blind in one eye, which he said was caused by a gun backfiring and exploding near his face when he was a young man. He also had a large, unfinished tribal scar that reached halfway across his upper chest, unlike the ones of the other men such as Georgie and Banjo, who had two or three lines that reached right across their chests. The scar looked as if it had been brought to an abrupt end; however, I never asked Sandy how or why this had happened. It was common for most of the men to have at least two or three tribal scars across their chests and along their upper arms. It was men's business and never discussed.

Sandy walked tall and proud, was a softly spoken and gentle man. He was not the traditional head stockman ogre who drove his men to the edge of survival and sanity. He never married or had children and he treated Billy and me like his own. He showed us how to ride properly and take care of our horses and saddles, how to plait a belt and make green hide ropes. When we were allowed to go out to the stock camp at night, we slept in our swags beside him, away from the rest of the stockmen.

He loved country music and had a little transistor radio with a long wire aerial that he threw up into a tree to listen to the Country and Western Radio Show from Mt Isa, Queensland. People from stations and road camps across the Top End wrote in requesting their favourite song be played, and sent messages to family and friends. This was one of the highlights of our lives, as we learnt new songs, heard old songs and, on a very rare occasion, heard a message for someone at Killarney.

Sandy happily passed on his bush skills to the many young stockmen who came and went. He knew how to break in a wild horse, castrate a bull, make saddles and bridles and plait beautiful belts and whips. He knew how to mend a fence and fix a bore, how to change a tyre and drive a truck. He had a deep understanding of the land and compassion and respect for the people around him.

When we went mustering, Sandy would show us what tracks belonged to which animal and how to tell if the tracks were old or new. He would kneel in the dirt and trace the track gently with a finger. 'See the sharp edges of this goanna track, that means they are new tracks, maybe about two or three hours old, and he is going for a drink at the creek. See these horse tracks, the edges are smoothed by the wind and they are underneath the goanna track so they are older, maybe the horses went for a drink early in the morning, before the goanna woke up.'

As we walked along behind the cattle, Sandy would tell us stories of when he was a little boy and how he had learnt to ride, track and mend saddles. He would talk about droving and the people he had met along the way. He had a wicked sense of humour and told stories of mad cooks, drovers and wild horses, amongst other things.

I was often perplexed by these stories but I understood that his was a complex culture. What seemed to me to be very cruel – stories of fighting with sticks and boomerangs and the payback system of spearing people for their misde-meanours – also gave me an awareness and understanding at a very young age of the complexities and rituals of another culture. I feel blessed and privileged that I had the opportunity to be included in a way most Australians are not. This was also due to my mother liking and enjoying the company of the Aboriginal people who lived with us on the station. We were not segregated, as per the social expectations of those times. We had sleepovers at the camp and the Aboriginal kids had sleepovers at our house.

Generally, though, Sandy spoke little about his tradi-tional life, nor did he mix with the full-blood Aboriginal people on the station. He loved to read paperback Western novels featuring 'Larry and Stretch' and listen to Slim Dusty and Charley Pride songs on a tape recorder. I don't recall him leaving the station much to visit his family – Killarney was his home. As he got older and retired as the head stockman, he took on the easier jobs of driving around checking fences and bores and managing the butcher shop.

Sandy didn't know what year he was born but I think he was most likely in his mid to late fifties when he sadly died, very quickly, of cancer, in the late 1980s. Sandy is buried with his brother Ringer Shaw and mother, where he grew up on Victoria River Downs Station.

Chapter 10

A BUSH EDUCATION

MY EDUCATION WAS AN ERRATIC AFFAIR IN THE FIRST few years, thanks to our numerous moves before setting up a permanent home. I learnt reading and writing from Mum as a day-to-day thing rather than from any formal lessons, until we were finally signed up to the South Australian Correspondence School when I was about seven or eight, and received structured sets of lessons that arrived in the mail every few months. We didn't have a regular mail service so relied on the Flying Doctor, travelling nurses and truck drivers to deliver the mail for us.

In our very first schoolroom we sat at a handmade table on empty upturned 5-gallon kerosene tins. The school days were erratic as Mum had so much to do. However, I somehow learnt to read and write. I treasured the lessons from the Correspondence School and loved the simple drawings and lined pages, and took huge pride in the set exercises, adding up and taking away numbers in arithmetic, spelling words and writing their meaning beside them and copying the cursive writing so they were an exact image of the ones on the sample page. I loved the compulsory readers; once I'd read them, they were sent off bearing my mother's signature to verify that I really had done the work. I always waited in great anticipation for the next lot. I consumed the stories featuring Dick, Dora, Nip and Fluff as fast as I could and before long was reading *Grimm's Fairy Tales*, Enid Blyton, *Black Beauty*, *Huckleberry Finn*, *The Arabian Nights* and *Sleeping Beauty* as well as the paperback cowboy and detective novellas that the stockmen read. My grandmother Lillian Tindill always sent lots of children's books for us to read.

Mail day was one of the most exciting days on the station for me and I could not wait to get my schoolwork back. I loved to read the neatly written comments by the unknown teacher 3000 kilometres away in Adelaide. She would stamp pictures of koalas, echidnas, platypus and kangaroos and the words 'excellent' or 'well done' onto the completed work. She wrote encouraging sentences such as, 'This is a lovely story about the donkey eating all the bread. I look forward to hearing more.'

A regular contributor to our reading and writing material was the Salvation Army Minister Captain Victor Pedersen, who flew a tiny Tiger Moth plane that looked like it was held together by sheets of paper and calico. Captain Pedersen always brought a supply of books and magazines for Mum and colouring books and pencils for us kids, along with a generous dose of the good Lord's word. We were given little cards of scriptures that we had to learn off by heart and recite to him on his next visit. He only visited once or twice a year and though I kept the little cards, I do not think I ever remembered one single line. The captain was a kindly man who loved his work and who persevered with us, knowing that my mother was a proclaimed atheist and it was up to him to do everything he could to save us from the clutches of the devil.

Captain Pedersen often brought films, which he set up and projected onto the back wall of our house. We would sit on blankets on the ground with the whole community – including the cook, the bore runner, the mechanic and the stockmen – to watch scratchy black-and-white reel-to-reel movies that often had an insect bustling around behind the lens. The projector would regularly get too hot and at the crucial moment the film would begin to burn around the edges and then melt as we watched it all happening on the wall. Everyone would groan with disappointment and wait patiently until he made repairs, which meant the story jumped from the middle of a scene to a completely different one because the damaged piece of film had been cut out and the remainder stuck back together with clear sticky tape.

My parents must have decided that we needed a little more disciplined learning as Mum was so busy with station life, so they sent Billy and me to board with Uncle Rex and Aunty Pat in Darwin in 1964, when I was nine. We were to attend school with their two little boys, Alan and Colin. Rex and Pat lived in a low-set brick house in a seaside suburb and we attended Nightcliff Primary School. We were glad to still be with family, as there was that same sense of humour, that same sense of belonging, that same little safety net – although, looking back, I wonder why anyone would put their kids in a cattle truck and send them to Darwin for school.

I don't remember a great deal about that year in Darwin other than that we played a lot on the crushed-ant-bed tennis court in the backyard and rode bikes up and down the street, but I do remember that this was the time I learnt to love cheese and Vegemite sandwiches. I took to school with great enthusiasm and after a few weeks in Grade 1 to determine my level, I was placed in Grade 3.

Darwin was a sprawling tropical town with wide roads and houses built on stilts. One of the biggest community events at the time was the annual *NT News* Walkabout, which was a sixteen-mile-long walk that most of the Darwin population participated in. Leading up to the competition, Aunty Pat took us to the football oval every evening to walk around for at least an hour. On the day of the competition, we packed early to drive out of town to the starting line. I completed the full sixteen miles in bare feet, shedding my sandshoes very early in the race, and came first in my age group. I carried the little trophy I won everywhere for over forty years.

Billy and I stayed the full year in Darwin but it may have been too stressful for my aunty or maybe my parents weren't able to pay for us to continue to stay up there, so the following year we stayed at home the first half of the year, doing correspondence. But we were dropping behind as Mum had so many children and much to do on the station, so we were sent to Katherine to live with Mum's youngest sister, Sue, and her husband, Barry, to attend the Katherine Area School. I was moved straight into Grade 6, which caught me up with my age group. I loved the school and my classes. I kept my pencils sharp and wrote neat cursive words, exactly within the lines, onto the crisp white pages of my schoolbooks. My love of school paid off and, at the end of the year, I was presented with a book as Dux of Grade 6. I still have that book, one of the few precious things I saved when our house was flooded in the Katherine Australia Day flood of 1998. My *NT News* Walkabout trophy, however, was lost.

The time with Aunty Sue was great and we liked being in Katherine because we knew everyone and felt more at home; however, it was most likely a stressful time for her to have two wild bush kids in her house with a new husband and baby, so the following year we stayed on Killarney again. This of course suited us very well as we loved being home on the station. During this time, Bill Tapp began to build a brick schoolhouse a few hundred metres away from our home. The schoolhouse had a small residence attached to it so my parents could employ a governess to cater for the growing student numbers being produced by my mother and the Aboriginal women.

Our ever-growing family provided a sure line-up of new students for the schoolroom. My little sister Shing soon joined us. Shing perched on her kerosene drum on her first day of school, hair brushed and face clean to begin the first page of Set 1 for Grade 1. Mum read out all the instructions and explained what was to be done for the day. She told Shing to, 'put a tick beside the right answer and a cross beside the wrong answer'.

Shing worked quietly and enthusiastically, as did Billy and I. Well, actually, I do not think Billy was ever enthusiastic and only did the bare minimum so he could get out of the schoolroom as quickly as possible to go to the cattle yards.

Mum returned to check our work and asked Shing how she was going. Shing proudly displayed her beautifully completed page. Crosses were placed in all the appropriate boxes, and little round cattle ticks with eight legs and two eyes were neatly placed in all the remaining boxes. That was Shing's version of a tick and why would she think anything different? We laughed and laughed and retold the story many times. It is still one of our favourite family stories.

—

Our first governess, Beth Marsh, was employed from Brisbane. She was very strict and loved bush poetry. She also loved the bush life, so she settled well into the station. Billy and I would go riding with Beth, who was intent on teaching us to ride 'properly', meaning like city hack riders. We took no heed, of course, and continued to gallop around at full speed, legs and arms flailing. While she was instructing us about sitting up straight, keeping toes pointed to the front and the reins held just so, she would make us recite Banjo Paterson and Henry Lawson poems. Billy hated it and tried to avoid going riding with her whenever he could. I was not very keen either and while I tried my best to learn the poems, I too avoided riding with her as much as I could.

Beth lived in the new school complex, which, like our house, had dirt floors, no doors or windows, no electricity and no running water. She taught a class of about six children in the schoolroom, with its wooden bookcase, chest of drawers and blackboard on the wall. She was very strict, which meant the boys were always skipping school. They would go up to the yards at smoko time and not return. Beth would complain to Bill Tapp and he would smile and give the kids a very lame lecture about the importance of school, but mostly he was to blame because he would give them some work while they were there and that provided an excuse not to return. A few hours at school in the morning was more than enough for the wild bush kids who did not want to be there.

Beth fell in love with our very handsome head stockman, Dave Mills, who was saving to buy his own cattle station. Dave loved bush poetry and rum and was able to consume copious amounts of both. Beth and Dave were married on the front verandah of our house in August 1968 and I, aged twelve, was chosen to be one of the flower girls. This was one of the most exciting things that had ever happened to me. I had never seen a wedding and did not own a dress. My measurements were sent off to some strange person in Brisbane and, lo and behold, just like magic, this piece of paper was transformed into the most beautiful fuchsia pink princess-line dress I had ever seen in my life. The dress came on the mail plane with Beth's full-length white lace dress with veil, silk bouquet and white high-heeled shoes. I felt like a princess and danced around on the dirt dance floor all night in my glorious dress with the white lace trim under the bodice, matching silk flower bouquet and a spray of flowers in my hair.

At the time of the wedding, we also had a rat plague. I do not know why there were millions of fat, grey rats invading the country but I do know that they ate everything in their path, including my beautiful pink dress. The morning after the wedding, I picked my dress up from beside the bed and it had raggedy holes chewed right into the front of it. I was devastated. I had dreamt of wearing it to every party on the station for the rest of my life!

The little school eventually received cement floors, doors and louvred windows. By the end of my primary schooling, Billy and I shared the classroom with our younger siblings, Shing, Sam and Joe, and some of the young Aboriginal children.

I did Grade 8 by correspondence before being told at the end of 1969 that Billy and I would be sent to boarding school the following year; Grade 8 by correspondence had not been very successful so I was to repeat the year down south. I found it difficult learning subjects like science from a page and languages like Latin and French were worlds away from what I was living and experiencing. Most of it made no sense at all. I was far better at speaking Mutburra, the local Indigenous language.

All the time that I was being home schooled, there was still work to do. I'd do anything that needed doing, because everyone worked on Killarney, regardless of age. I'd work in the cattle yards, helping with the drafting and branding of the animals. I'd go out on musters. I'd clean the houses, and look after the kids, just as I always had.

A lot of people might think us kids should have been allowed to be kids but I never saw any of these jobs as work – it was just life. And it was fun. I loved being busy, loved helping the adults with the many tasks that had to be done. I wanted to be like the adults – they were our role models. They were people who worked hard and lived passionately; people who kept a community going and who cared about each other. We never for a second felt like we weren't valued or that we didn't have an important role to play. Maybe that was part of the genius of the way Bill Tapp and Mum ran the place: everyone felt like they belonged, everyone felt like they were worth something. It could be a difficult place – the seasons alone saw to that – but it was a place where everyone lived life fully. Not many kids get to grow up like that.

Chapter 11

BOARDING SCHOOL DAYS

I HAD JUST TURNED FOURTEEN AND WAS NOT VERY HAPPY about having to leave home to go to a strange school out of the Northern Territory. Bill Tapp's mother, Sarah Tapp, had retired to the Gold Coast so it was decided that Billy and I would go to the coeducational school of Scots College and Presbyterian Girls College (PGC) in Warwick, Queensland. It meant we grandchildren could be close to our step-grandmother, whom we called Gram, and we could attend a school that was equivalent to the Scots College in Sydney that Bill Tapp had attended. We were waved off to boarding school on a road-train full of wild bulls and virtually empty suitcases, as we did not have any clothing that would be suitable for the flash city life, and we did not own things such as pyjamas, socks, or any winter gear. This would all be purchased on arrival at school along with uniforms and other essentials.

The road-train driver delivered us and the load of cattle to Darwin some twelve hours later, and we caught a TAA plane directly to Brisbane. We had travelled on the Connellans' mail plane on the odd occasion when going to school in Darwin; however, we had never been on a big passenger airplane, nor had we ever stayed in a nice motel room. On the plane trip, we thought we were so sophisticated when we were handed a meal in a white glass dish with shiny stainless-steel knives and forks, linen serviettes and china teacup and saucer. Those were the days when real crockery and cutlery were standard on the aircraft and everyone smoked, including us as we got older. We lifted the lid off the meal and after discussion about what some of the vegetables could possibly be, and who was game to try them first, we decided that we knew what the purple grape in the side salad was. We both popped the grape into our mouths at the same time. We spluttered and winced and looked at each other in disgust. It was a salty, sour olive. It took me many years to try one again and Billy still will not eat them.

A manager from the stock and station company Elders Goldsborough Mort (Elders GM) picked us up at the

airport and took us to an upmarket hotel in the middle of
Brisbane. Our heads swivelled like the clowns in sideshow
alley as we drove through the city. Thousands of cars
whizzed by and there were traffic lights and traffic jams,
high-rise buildings and dazzling shop fronts and millions
of white people. We had never eaten in a restaurant or even
a decent café until that night. Billy and I sat in the motel
restaurant with white linen tablecloths and gleaming wine
glasses as the waiter took our orders. We ordered steak and
vegetables because we had no idea what half the things
on the menu were. In 1970, Katherine had a population
of 2500 and still did not have television.

The following day Gram picked us up from the hotel in
her little silver Volkswagen and took us back to the Gold
Coast for the weekend. A well-off woman in her own
right, she lived in a spacious new brick home right on the
waterfront on the Isle of Capri. Gram visited Killarney
every year and we had seen photos of her home and the
beaches when we had slide nights. Our grandmother could
not wait to get us into a good hot bath and buy us some
new clothes.

I felt very awkward and out of my depth. I had spent
most of my life until then in a swag and I was overwhelmed
by the beautiful bedroom with crisp white cotton sheets
and a floral bedspread. Delicate lace doilies sat beneath
exquisite porcelain figurines and a Tiffany bedside lamp.

I had only ever seen such things in books. I crept carefully into the white linen sheets with my crusty brown feet, wearing the first pair of pyjamas I had ever owned. I had never slept in a room by myself, without my family close around me.

My little world was expanding rapidly and nothing prepared me for the overwhelming homesickness, for feeling different and out of depth in those first months at my new school. Everything was so foreign. I did not talk much, I just did as I was told. As I was fitted out with a nametag and bottle-green school bag full of books that I had never seen, I wondered how I could get out of there and get home. Tears sat under my eyelids and I felt so lonely and out of my depth. I couldn't fathom the strictness and routine; the idea of having to wear uniforms with the hem exactly 2 inches above the knee and long brown socks pulled up to my knees were only two of the strange things required of me. The bells echoed through the old wooden boarding house to get up in the morning, to go to breakfast, to catch the bus; to go to sport, to eat dinner and to do homework, and to go to bed. I hated those bells. The summer uniform was a blue–green tartan cotton shift with a woven panama hat. There were black shoes that had to be polished every afternoon. On Sundays, we had to walk the few blocks to the Presbyterian church in our white linen suits, stockings, black shoes and panama hats.

This was the first year that PGC and Scots had amalgamated as a coeducational school and all lessons were held at Scots College. I couldn't wait to go over to Scots for lessons each day so I could see Billy and feel some connection to home. Our school also went over to Scots for socials, movies and sports days, so there were other opportunities to see the brother I was so used to seeing all the time, every day.

The first term ticked away like each day was forty-eight hours long. I cried on my bed every afternoon and sobbed with a pillow over my head far into the night. I marched to meals in the dining room, where I was allocated a seat at a long, white linen–covered table, with a Year 12 Senior and a housemistress. I didn't know what cutlery to use and ate very little in those first weeks as I watched from under lowered lids to see how people ate. The food was foreign and I hated sago and porridge, but loved the fresh bread, butter and honey. I craved a big juicy steak, salty corned beef and rib bones cooked on the open fire.

I missed Killarney so much it was physical. The first three months of first term felt like three years. I eagerly waited for the long letters from my mum, who wrote in depth about what everyone at home was doing, how many cattle were mustered, whose birthday it was and who had been sick, or who'd had a fight and left the station. I loved letter-writing time on Saturday morning, when I could write home and tell my mum how much I hated school and how I had to get out of there before I died.

The first school holidays finally arrived and as Billy and I flew into Darwin, looking at the stunning, flat, dry season landscape out of the plane window, I felt the weight of sadness lift off my chest. I could not wait to see my cousins and aunty in Darwin and my nana in Katherine on my way home. In the car, every mile seemed to take forever, but we chattered excitedly as the landmarks flew by the window and finally the signpost came into view: KILLARNEY 42. We were home; we knew every inch of that winding dirt track and were happy to open the five gates, the ones that we had fought over before boarding school days because no one ever wanted to open them. As the station came into view, I cried with happiness and swore I was never leaving again, no matter what Mum or Bill Tapp said. I would kill myself first, I declared.

We flew out of the car into the house – 'Hello, Mum, we're home.' We threw our cases on the beds and headed up to the cattle yards to see everyone and to make sure everything else was the same. Bill Tapp was still in the office on the phone, Mum still had a tea towel over her shoulder and a cigarette in her hand. There was our Aboriginal house help, Nancy Holtze, hanging out the washing and kids running in and out of the house, just as they always did. The dust still hung thick over the cattle yards as the cattle bawled and the stockmen banged gates and slammed the red branding iron. My horse was still there and my saddle was hanging where it always hung. Old Micko was still in the kitchen and Pat and Tom Quirk had their heads under a Toyota bonnet. The handsome young stockmen were still laughing, teasing and skylarking and the old women were still at the camp. I felt like I had died and gone to heaven. My home hadn't disappeared while I was living in another part of the universe.

That night we had a family dinner at home, all eight children – Caroline had been born in June 1968 – and Mum and Bill Tapp, feasting on a bubbling beef stew and heaps of mashed potato as we laughed and I bragged about school and how we had to wear pyjamas and dressing gowns and socks, and ribbons in our hair.

Billy and I filled the days with working in the yards, riding with cattle, drafting and branding, and swimming in the muddy dams. We ate in the men's dining room and sat outside at night, catching up on all the stories, playing guitars and singing country and western songs.

The three weeks of school holidays came and went too quickly and before we knew it we were back on a cattle truck heading to Darwin and back to school. I cried for the entire day before leaving and halfway to town. I still hated the school but it wasn't so scary now that I knew how the routines worked and realised that I had made a couple of friends, who had been just as homesick as I was.

I arrived back at school for second term in May and was given a new uniform to wear for winter: tartan wool kilt, flannelette shirts, bottle-green tights, singlets, blazers, long pyjamas and woolly dressing gown and slippers. We slept in long dormitories, fifteen beds down each side. The cold came in with a vengeance as the wind whipped up through the floorboards, through gaping doors into the Queenslander-style building, designed for a tropical climate. One of my friends lent me her spare hot water bottle until I was able to buy one.

Billy, just twelve years old, told me it was freezing in the junior boys dormitory at Scots, that there was ice on the pipes and that he had to go through the initiation ceremonies: having the 'Royal Flush' – one's head flushed in the toilet – and being locked in the large dirty-washing boxes filled with socks and underpants, with the older boys sitting on top. Thankfully, there did not seem to be any initiation ceremonies at PGC, although there was a very distinctive pecking order between the grades and the power and authority of the senior girls and prefects.

For most of Year 8 I felt out of my depth and weird. No one knew anything about the Northern Territory and one of the boys at school used to call me a 'boong'. I couldn't fathom what this meant until I asked him in later years why he'd called me that. He said he'd thought that all Territorians were called 'boongs'. In Year 9 I settled in and, despite the yearning to be at home, I began to enjoy my time at boarding school, as I loved fashion, dance, art and music, and boarding school gave me an opportunity to pursue my interests in those things. It was very different to living under a cloud of dust and mustering cattle.

I had made friends with Janet Dowling, whose parents worked in Papua New Guinea for the Federal Government. We were both incredibly homesick; we understood each other's isolation, and how different our home lives were from those of mainstream Australia. Janet's parents had separated and she was far from home, and miserable with it. When she decided to run away to Sydney to see her father, I told her I would go with her. We planned for a week how and when we would leave. The old boarding house was not very secure and quite easy to get out of. We often sat on the back steps at night and smoked, so we knew we could leave undetected.

One evening we packed our school bags, set our alarms for midnight and went to bed in tracksuits. At the stroke of midnight, we left our beds and snuck through the creaking dormitory and out the back door, then down onto the railway line to begin our journey to Sydney. We walked along the railway line until we came to the road to the little township of Killarney, which in my fanciful teenage mind was a sign that this was a trip home. Killarney was near the New South Wales border, and heading in the right direction to get to Sydney. I hadn't thought about how I was going to get home to the Northern Territory from Sydney, I just assumed that Janet's father would sort that out when we got there. It was a freezing winter night and there were not a lot of cars on the road. We agreed that we would only try to flag down a car if we could see that there were two people in it, so every time a car came by with one person, we dived into the table drain to hide.

After a few kilometres in the freezing cold, I was wondering whether this was such a good idea – we were both just fifteen and I had never been to Sydney. Finally, a car came by with a couple in it and we stepped out with our thumbs out to hitch a ride. The car slowed down and the man in the front seat asked us where we were going.

'Sydney,' we replied.

'Well, we're going to Killarney, the little township just south of Warwick, where we live,' he said, 'and it's a very cold night. I think you should come home with us for the night and then we will discuss how you can get to Sydney in the morning.'

As we were driving down the highway, the man said to me, 'Do you come from a cattle station in the Northern Territory?'

Without thinking I said, 'Yes, Killarney Station.'

'You're one of the Tapp children, aren't you?'

I could not believe what I was hearing – did this man have ESP?

'How do you know that?'

'I delivered a truck-load of hay and horse feed to Killarney in May. I remember meeting you kids at the men's dining room for dinner, you telling me you went to boarding school in Warwick.'

I couldn't deny it, and I didn't know if I was happy that we were warm and safe or unhappy about being discovered on a lonely road with my friend Janet on my way to Sydney.

At breakfast time they said they would have to ring the boarding school to tell them where we were, as they were sure everyone would have been worried about us. Then they'd return us to Warwick.

We had not considered the risks or the ruckus we would cause and arrived back at the boarding school to meet a very angry and very relieved headmistress. She had called the police, who were out looking for us. By then both sets of parents had been alerted that we were missing and we had to call and talk to them. I rarely phoned home as the radio telephone network in the NT was limited and hard to hear over. I eventually got through to my mother, who didn't seem too worried; I'd spent more dangerous nights away in the stock camp, camping with wild cattle and dingoes prowling the perimeter.

Typical of my mum, as I was about to hang up she laughed and said, 'You didn't get very far! Write me a letter and tell me all about it.'

I was given detention and wasn't able to go on school trips or to socials for the rest of the term. Janet's father came to the school and took her home, and I never saw her again. I was terribly upset at losing my friend in much the same way as I'd lost Nita: with no warning, and no chance to say goodbye.

***

I settled into my two lives after the attempt to run away and began to enjoy being a girl and doing the girl things I couldn't do at home. I loved dancing and created dance routines for our end-of-year school concert. I joined the school magazine committee and collected stories and took photos for it, and joined the choir to sing at church and other functions in the town. I played the guitar and held séances in the middle of the night, which was a school tradition (apparently). I took part in sport because I had to – hockey, athletics and netball – but I was not particularly good at it because I didn't like getting up early for training. I did enjoy the swimming team and excelled at one-metre diving; I represented the school in the Southern Queensland Championships; however, I think this was more to do with the gorgeous blond-haired trainer than the actual diving.

My parents came to visit only twice in the four years I was at school. The first time they drove into the school in a shining white Ford LTD with the sun roof open. Mum swept out of the car in a flowing dress, a big sun hat and cigarette in hand. She won the staff over in no time with her vivacious personality, and she and Bill Tapp took me and Billy to the Gold Coast for the weekend. Mum and I went on a shopping spree to the boutiques and I returned to school with the latest outfits, which included a crocheted bikini, long hippy dress, bell-sleeve shirts, flared jeans, platform shoes and a pair of knee-high brown leather boots. Nothing practical, of course, like winter underwear, jackets and jumpers, but I didn't care and nor did Mum.

Chapter 12

IT'S A NEW WORLD

WE DID NOT HAVE TV IN THE NORTHERN TERRITORY – and because we didn't have it, we didn't know what we were missing out on. We didn't watch a lot of TV at school, either, although my favourite show was *Young Talent Time* with Johnny Young on a Saturday evening. I played the guitar and sang my heart out every day after school, practising for my spot on that show. I never did get it, but I'd done enough singing round the camp fire at home at Killarney to rate myself as a singer. Everyone sang at Killarney – it was just what you did.

Mum was a prolific writer of letters to the editor to all the big southern newspapers – *The Nation Review, The*

Australian, *The Age*, *The Bulletin* and many others – so a number of my school teachers were aware of her politics and the fight for issues such as land rights, equality and self-government. A teacher would often tell me they had seen a letter of Mum's in one of the national papers. My mother's political activism was being recorded regularly in the Territory media at the time that land rights were coming to the notice of the rest of Australia. When Mum was invited to be a guest of Gerald Stone on the premier political show of the time, *This Day Tonight*, my house-mistress asked if I would like to leave homework time early and watch it with some of the teachers and my school friends. I jumped at the chance and was thrilled to see my mother on TV.

As Mum railed about the inequity of Territorians being ruled from Canberra by people who had never been to the Northern Territory, and the fear that Aboriginal land rights would cripple the growth of the NT and the cattle industry – all the time chain-smoking, her electric-blue eyes flashing and her passion for justice clearly on display – I felt so proud of her. This was typical of the forthright people I was used to – people like my mum standing up for the Territory. I am not too sure what the teachers thought, but no doubt they were a little shocked and maybe understood my rebellious nature a little better.

I didn't do a lot of school work in my years at PGC, just enough to get by, though I loved art and English and did well at these. I was popular with the boys and in Year 11 snuck out at night to meet them on the railway line, to smoke and enjoy long, passionate kisses and lots of groping on the bitterly cold nights.

My brother Billy told me that he never had the same intensity of homesickness that I did. Though he missed home terribly, he had good mates and loved the team sports that he could not participate in at home, in particular football and cricket.

Through my years at boarding school, I rarely went with friends to their homes for the school holidays – I never wanted to miss going home to Killarney. It was also during these visits that I began to notice that Bill Tapp was drinking more and that he and Mum were fighting all the time.

The bigwigs of Elders GM made regular trips to Killarney to witness the results of their lending. Killarney was hitting the heights of being the pastoral industry trendsetter while I was at school. Cattle prices were good and Bill Tapp was spending up big on stud cattle and horses and flash cars. The social life that went with attending sales and functions down south increased his anxiety and his drinking.

As his drinking took hold, he became more and more obsessive and would ring people at all hours of the day and night to repeat conversations over and over again. He would worry about what he had said when he was drunk and then apologise repeatedly, constantly reiterating what he had said and what he meant and how he hadn't intended to hurt anyone.

Mum said that he kept her awake, sometimes all night, rehashing conversations, repeatedly seeking reassurance that he had said the right thing or made the right decision.

No one ever was sacked from Killarney, as Bill Tapp did not want to hurt people's feelings. And there were some very sackable offences committed, some that people should have been jailed for, such as stealing a vehicle to go on a grog run to the nearest roadhouse, rolling and damaging vehicles and equipment through carelessness, wife-bashing, stealing and assault. Still, Bill Tapp would not send the offenders away.

Though most often quite stern and serious, Bill Tapp was a lot of fun as well and loved sitting on the front verandah at night with a few drinks and us kids. My cousins from Darwin would come out to visit most school holidays and Robyn and I would sing songs for him. We set up the cassette player, painstakingly wrote out the words to each song in a songbook, and then practised singing them. Robyn was a great guitar player and I did the singing. Bill Tapp's favourites were Roy Orbison and Slim Dusty and Mum's was Patsy Cline. There was very little variety from country music. Jim Reeves, Charley Pride and Marty Robbins peppered with pop music by Cliff Richards and the Beatles and a bit of Al Martino and Frank Sinatra.

It was while I was at boarding school that an eight-year-old Aboriginal boy was accidentally shot and killed when two of my young brothers and their Aboriginal friends, Irene and Danny, went for a drive out to a nearby paddock to get firewood and look for a bush turkey for dinner for the Aboriginal camp. Danny had only been at Killarney for a few weeks, having returned from the Katherine Show with his uncle, who worked for us.

All the station vehicles had guns in them, either a .303 or .22 calibre slung between the driver's seat and gearbox or on steel hooks welded to the front of the dashboard behind the steering wheel. There was always a packet of bullets in the glove box. The guns were used for getting a killer, our weekly supply of beef, and shooting snakes or dingoes that attacked weakened cows and their calves or other weak or distressed animals

The three boys had gotten out of the vehicle and the Aboriginal girl, Danny's cousin Irene, was sitting in the front of the 'bull catcher', a modified short wheelbase vehicle with the roof, sides and doors removed. Irene picked up the gun and pointed it and said, 'Don't move or I will shoot you.'

Danny moved and she pulled the trigger and shot him in the side.

The kids, shocked, all jumped into the vehicle and sped home, leaving Danny's bleeding body dead on the ground.

They didn't tell anyone what had happened until Mum, sensing something different with my two brothers, asked why they were home so early and what was wrong. Initially they said nothing but under more questioning they told what had happened. By this time, the Aboriginal people had also realised the situation when they questioned Irene as to why she was crying so much.

A group of stockmen went out to the paddock and picked up the little body, wrapped him in a blanket and put him in the air-conditioned vet room at the cattle yards to await the arrival of the police, who had to travel from Katherine.

My brothers remember being questioned for what seemed like hours by the police in the station office, without an adult in the room. They repeated their stories over and over, as did little Irene. Finally the police took the boy's body to Katherine to be buried by his family. It was obvious that this was an accident. Thing had gone tragically wrong when a few kids set out to have an afternoon of fun.

It was a traumatic time for everyone on the station, and Irene's father Jimmy was terrified of payback for her and himself, by the family of the dead boy. Jimmy wore a red bandana as a sign of his mourning and when it came time for everyone to leave for the Christmas break he would not send Irene into Katherine to the extended family for fear of payback.

My brother Daniel was born in 1971. Mum timed it well because I was home on school holidays. Her final and tenth child, Kate, was born in December 1973, a few weeks after I had finished school in Year 11. When Mum was pregnant, Bill Tapp would say, 'I'm taking Mum to town to have a baby,' and she'd simply waft off to town and come back with a new baby. Mum said she virtually only ever made it in the door in time for most of them. Back then it would have been a four- or five-hour drive to town, and it was rough on those dirt roads. Daniel and Kate were both born during the Wet so there was the worry that an uncrossable swollen river or getting bogged could mean the baby being born on the side of the road. Somehow luck was always on their side and Mum made it to hospital in time.

That final wet season school holidays, when Kate was born, I was able to convince Bill Tapp that I would be more use at home working in the office than returning for Year 12. While most of my friends seemed to know what careers they would follow when they left school, I didn't know what I wanted to do, other than be home at Killarney. My duties included answering the phone, typing letters and filing, helping to look after the general medical issues: doling out antiseptic cream, ear and eye drops, bandages and antibiotics. I opened the store every evening before dinner for everyone to get their beer, tobacco and other personal items. As always, there was plenty of washing and cleaning, and helping Mum with whatever had to be done, including looking after my little blue-eyed brother Daniel and baby sister Kate.

The wet season of 1974 was one of the biggest ever recorded, with the Coolibah Creek the highest we had ever seen it. Floodwaters snuck up into the back garden and Bill Tapp decided to empty the house of furniture.

They brought the cattle truck up to the front door and emptied the house of fridges and household goods, linen and mattresses and stored them all in the big hay shed. The water kept creeping towards the back door and lapped up the single step. It swirled through my room and the laundry and we anxiously waited to see if it would flow into the house. Time seemed to stand still and then the water level slowly dropped, leaving in its wake downed power lines, wrecked fences and waterlogged bore pumps.

Once the water had receded we had to get the power lines back up for the bore down at the creek so fresh water could flow back to the station water supply tank.

Bill Tapp and Ivan Woods and another worker went down the back of the house with the tractor to start pulling the power poles upright and re-hang the power lines onto to them. I was in the laundry hanging out wet clothes when I heard a gut-wrenching scream and saw Bill Tapp loping through the thick black soil mud towards the house. He was running towards the power house to shut down the engines about another 300 metres away and he was calling, 'Ivan's been electrocuted, Ivan's been electrocuted.' I raced down towards the creek to find Ivan all purple, lying in the mud, and the young fellow, who was only about sixteen, confused and unsure of what to do. By this time people were converging from everywhere and the stud manager, John Hart, raced up, saying, 'Give him mouth-to-mouth.'

As it turned out, I had just completed my lifesaving Bronze Medal at school and knew what to do. I started mouth-to-mouth while John began instructing everyone on what else to do. Ivan lay warm and purple in the mud. Mum came racing down to see what was happening and returned to get blankets to wrap him in. John and I and the cook, Mrs Robbins, who had only been at Killarney for about eight weeks, shared the task of delivering mouth-to-mouth and heart massage. People gathered around, silent as we knelt in the mud, frantically trying to bring him back to life. I willed him to breathe, and kept asking Mrs Robbins if he had a pulse. By this time Bill Tapp had managed to turn all the generators off and get on the radio telephone to the doctor in Katherine.

Despite our trying resuscitation for what seemed like hours, Ivan did not respond. Bill Tapp went backwards and forwards to the phone with updates for the doctor, who eventually advised that it was unlikely Ivan could have survived, being damp and standing knee-deep in the mud when 240 volts went through him. Sandy Shaw brought a vehicle down with an old door to use as a stretcher and we placed Ivan, wrapped in his blanket, on the door and took his body on the back of the Toyota to a clean empty house.

We were flooded in and a plane could not land at Killarney due to the airstrip being too wet and boggy. Ivan would have to remain on the station till they could get there. All the emergency services helicopters were busy evacuating people out of flood situations across the region so could not come to pick up Ivan; he stayed in the house overnight.

There was little anyone could do but wait. The accident had happened in the late afternoon so everything came to a standstill. Most of us sat around in the recreation room quietly drinking tea, not knowing what to say, and after dinner we sat up late into the night, wondering how it had all gone so wrong.

Bill Tapp drowned his sorrows in a bottle of whisky. He blamed himself for not turning the whole of the station power off. He had turned off the power box that led to the bore. Ivan was picking up the power lines out of the mud when he hit a live wire, a spot where the cockatoos had chewed through the outer plastic tubing.

The following day an emergency services helicopter landed in front of the recreation room with a policeman on board. As Bill Tapp was now well immersed in his drinking binge I took the policeman to the house and had to identify the body. The only evidence was the large burn on Ivan's hand. He looked perfect, as if in a deep sleep, and I wished he would just open his eyes and say that he was playing a big joke on us.

The policeman then asked Sandy to assist with putting Ivan into a white body bag and strapping it to the side of the helicopter. Everyone stood in silence as the helicopter fired up, lifted gently and disappeared into the dark stormy sky.

Ivan Woods had come to live with us when he was fourteen years old and was part of our family for many years. He had left Killarney to get married and returned in 1973. He was incredibly fit and daring and could do standing backflips and walk on his hands. Though virtually illiterate, he was smart and everyone liked him. He didn't know the word fear and would throw wild bulls and ride the roughest horse in the stock camp. He would put on buckjumping displays that had us holding our breath and I don't ever remember seeing him get thrown. He was a show-off and an actor and I loved him for it. Ivan was handsome and had a cocky walk; he could get up a great John Wayne swagger. I just thought he was the best and cleverest person in the world. He broke in his own horse, a beautiful brown with a big white blaze and four white feet, and called him Thunderbolt. I thought that was the best name ever given to a horse, especially as ours had boring names like Blue Bob, Billy Boy and Blackie.

Ivan was taken at the age of twenty-three. He had been a part of the growing-up of Killarney for almost a decade and he left a big hole in our lives.

My life changed on that day, the thirteenth of March 1974. I was no longer a kid. I was eighteen years of age, a responsible adult who had to step up to the plate. I had experienced the need for survival and the deaths of animals almost on a daily basis but the tenuous line between life and death hits home hard when you witness the death of someone so young and so close to you. One foot put wrong and in an instant, it can all be over.

The cattle industry was in the doldrums then, putting a lot of financial pressure on Bill Tapp. The cracks in my parents' marriage were widening, the fights getting more intense, screaming and yelling long into the night, doors slamming and things being thrown, and with Mum sporting bruises on her arms and spending nights sleeping out the back behind the banana trees.

One of the first pastoral field days in the Territory was held at Killarney, opening up the station to the public in 1972. The pastoralists came to listen and learn about the latest techniques in animal husbandry and cattle breeding, and to view the modern cattle yards and station complex. People travelled in their hundreds from across the Territory and interstate to attend the Killarney Field Days and, in later years, the famous Killarney quarter horse sales. The entertainment and the booze flowed freely.

Over 200 people listened to guest speakers, including the Deputy Chief Minister of Australia, Ian Sinclair, and leader of the NT Legislative Assembly, Goff Letts, at that first field day. Celebrities and politicians, including Nugget Coombs, Deputy Prime Minster Doug Anthony, Rex Paterson, Les MacFarlane, and the first Northern Territory Chief Minister, Paul Everingham, would all visit Killarney in its heyday during the 1970s and 1980s. In 1984, Thomas Keneally and his wife spent a week at Killarney photographing and writing, which led to a chapter on Killarney in his coffee table book, *Outback*. The intense interest in Killarney and the family resulted in a documentary about my brothers Billy, Joe, Ben, William and Daniel, *Unbroken Spirit,* made by Australian artist and documentary makers George Gittoes and Gabrielle Dalton, which aired on Discovery Channel USA, and the Seven Network in Australia. Print articles featured in most national newspapers and weeklies across Australia including *The Bulletin*, *The Sydney Morning Herald*, *New Idea*, *ITA*, *Post* and *Wellbeing.* Famous Australian author Colleen McCullough spent a week at Killarney filming, then presented a story on the ABC TV show *A Big Country* that won a Penguin Award for excellence in broadcasting in 1980. In it, McCullough said, 'When Bill Tapp is in the room, John Wayne isn't.'

Bill Tapp was living a large life, and he'd become larger than life. It wouldn't turn out to be a development that benefited him or any of us who loved him. Bill Tapp's legend might have been growing, but he was still the same obsessive, compulsively worrying man who had left his city life behind to pursue a big dream. Part of him certainly wanted that role – that renown – as a big Territory figure, while another part seemed to be collapsing under the weight of it.

Being Bill Tapp was a job for more than one person, no matter how strong or capable they were. But Bill Tapp would never ask for help – not even from Mum – and so he kept his concerns to himself, only letting them out when he got hold of a bottle. It wasn't a new story – and he wasn't the only man on Killarney to use grog to try to escape himself. It was hard, though – hard for him, hard for us.

Following the purchase of Quarter Commando, the foundation quarter horse stallion, and the Santa Gertrudis bull, King Ranch Oregon, both for Australian record prices in 1969, Bill Tapp needed to build a set of yards befitting their status. The new steel cattle yards covered five acres and could hold over 3000 head of cattle at one time. The streamlined yard designs allowed for the easy movement of stock. Lights were installed so that drafting could be carried out in the cool of the night to lessen the stress on the cattle and there was a large sprinkler system to settle the dust. Specialised yards were built for the stud cattle with a set of weighing scales and an air-conditioned room to store the semen for the artificial insemination programs and veterinary products.

Round yards were built for breaking in the new crop of young quarter horses for the Killarney stock camp and those that would be sold in annual auction sales to increase income to the station. A large grandstand and an auctioneer's box was built, along with a camp-drafting and cutting arena to train the horses that would go up for sale. There were concrete wash-down bays and a manicured lawn that ran the length of the stud and sale area.

A 500-metre avenue of fig trees welcomed visitors to Killarney. The sprawling modern brick buildings were like no others seen in the Territory. There were air-conditioned staff quarters and a new kitchen with guest dining room attached. A set of motel rooms catered for the constant flow of visiting government employees and guests. There was a large undercover recreation area and the station store that opened every night for essentials and two beers per person. There was even a big new chook house and a fence around the vegetable garden. Everything was built with purpose, precision and obsessive neatness.

The brothers Pat and Tom Quirk built the massive steel cattle yards. They lived and worked at Killarney for over twenty years. Pat was the more talkative of the two; Tom rarely spoke at all. The only discussion they seemed to have was about a vehicle they were fixing, or how to design a part to compensate for something that could not be brought in from town. Both were brilliant welders and motor mechanics. They could fix anything, such as bores, cars, cattle trucks and graders, and could build anything made from steel or wood.

Pat and Tom's parents managed the famous Victoria River Downs Station from which Killarney had been excised in the 1950s. They never really spoke about anything much, apart from saying that they'd gone to boarding school in Queensland. They went to one of those strict Catholic schools that treated boys like soldiers, but they never said anything bad about it. Both were bachelors, neither having ever married; I don't know if they'd had any relationships of any sort prior to their coming to Killarney. Mum remembers one of them having a girlfriend, but not a wife or children. The brothers initially lived in a tent away from the rest of the station people and then moved into a room with two single beds when the men's quarters were built. The brothers were heavy drinkers and smokers; they sat in the same seats at the same table in the men's dining room at beer time for twenty years. They occasionally left the station for a break – sometimes only every two or three years. During the breaks they stayed at a motel in Katherine in the same room, similar to the one at home, until they drank all their savings and returned to Killarney in the old Toyota they affectionately called 'Tojo'.

When they went on holiday, we would give their room a spring clean. We would find a year's supply of empty Log Cabin tobacco tins piled in one corner along with empty cigarette paper packets and Red Lady matchboxes. In another corner would be a pile of filthy navy blue trousers and shirts. They only bought new clothes three times a year, always the Hard Yakka brand. Mum would order them two new shirts, two pairs of trousers and one pair of boots each and they would wear these, unwashed, until they got a new set. Their shirts had large white sweat stains across the back and under the arms and the trousers were solid with black grease marks where they wiped their hands in the workshop. They never used sheets or pillowcases so every year we had to throw the mattresses out and buy new ones.

Pat and Tom never had any pets but somehow acquired two black crows that had fallen out of a nest when they were little. The crows, aptly named Heckle and Jeckle, followed the brothers to work each day, flying from rooftop to rooftop to the workshop. Throughout the day, they flew around the station, and returned to a tree near the recreation room at meal times when the bell rang.

Everyone liked to have conversations with the crows.

'How are you going, boys? What have you been up to today?'

'Hot bastard of a day today, hey? Even for a crow!'

Heckle and Jeckle would watch with great interest, nodding their heads as if they understood every word.

The crows were very smart and decided to play games with the humans. They would steal the keys out of the bull catcher vehicles, or steal a packet of tobacco off the outside table and take them to the roof. Pat and Tom would yell at them, 'Come on, boys – bring those keys back!'

Others would swear at them: 'I am going to wring your scrawny black neck when I get hold of you!'

The black birds would look down from the hot tin roof in amusement, cocking their heads one way and then the other way, a twinkle in their eye, daring you to come after them. Eventually, one of the younger people would be sent to get the ladder to climb up on the roof and retrieve the stolen goods.

For many years the much-loved birds were the cause of great entertainment, until one day Heckle died and, not long after, Jeckle committed harakiri by getting overly inquisitive. He stood on the edge of the washing machine and pecked at the red dot on the clothes roller, which squished the clothes from the machine into the rinsing tub. He got a little too close, his head was clamped in the roller and, sadly, that was the end of Jeckle.

Pat and Tom went into mourning; they did not speak for days, and afterwards always talked affectionately about the birds, as if they were favourite family members who had passed on.

As time passed, Tom became forgetful, vague and would wander off on his own. He was diagnosed with dementia by the visiting doctor and became more talkative as he began to move into his own world. He became known as 'Mad Tom'. No one took any notice of him. He went about his business in his own mind and continued to work with his brother on vehicles. He would walk past the packed table at beer time, having an animated discussion with himself, or he'd fire off something to the group: 'I know you're all quiet because I've given you all the sack,' he might say, to which of course everyone would burst into loud laughter. As he returned from picking up his beers from the store, he'd say, 'I am glad you're all happy because I'm going to reinstate you – you've all got a job now!'

Pat became more vigilant in looking after his brother and would say, 'You coming to get your beer now, Tom? You coming to dinner now, Tom? You coming to bed now, Tom?'

Tom always followed with a grunt.

Mum had discussions with the Flying Doctor and convinced Tom to see him. Tom was given some medication, but he slowly deteriorated, and when he began to scare the school teacher by telling everyone that she had a baby to him and it was hidden in the school room ceiling, it was time to consider finding him the right place to live where he would be cared for by the right people. Tom went to Katherine to live in the Red Cross home, but he deteriorated quite quickly while living there and died not long after he left Killarney.

One can only imagine how distressing this must have been for his brother and best mate, Pat, who never said a word about it. Pat died a few years after Tom, of a heart attack. Our family paid for their funerals in Katherine and placed a memorial plaque for them on the saddle shed wall in recognition of their great skills and contribution to Killarney at the cattle yards, which is still there today.

Chapter 13

ELIZABETH TAYLOR OF
THE OUTBACK

MY MOTHER HATES BEING CALLED THE 'ELIZABETH Taylor of the Outback', as she was dubbed by one local newspaper, but she has always been that and much more.

Five-foot-two with flashing blue eyes and long black hair, not only did she look like the beautiful Hollywood movie star but her marriage to Bill Tapp also mirrored those of the star and her actor husband, Richard Burton, with Mum's volatile temper, and raging arguments and fights between the couple happening both in public and behind closed doors. Mum and Bill Tapp had come together quickly and passionately, and that passion never faded – it just played out in different ways as they grew older and acquired more responsibilities.

My mother is outrageous and outspoken with a huge sense of humour and an insatiable quest for knowledge. She never stops learning and never stops finding a cause to champion. She is magnetic, outgoing, and able to laugh at herself. She also had ten children and two marriages in eighteen years, in the days before disposable nappies, packaged baby food, milk formulas and the contraceptive Pill.

Mum has lived her life with gusto, humour and an interest in everything and everyone. She has consumed books by the mountains, often reading the same book repeatedly if there was nothing else to hand. She read Tolstoy, Ayn Rand, Christina Stead, John Steinbeck, Kafka and Tolkien along with every newspaper and magazine she could. She would keep up with world news through crackly old Radio Australia, which always seemed to be at its worst when there was some earth-shattering news such as the assassination of US President John F Kennedy or the moon landing.

Mum was the opposite of Bill Tapp in every way. Bill Tapp did not like confrontation or offending anyone, which I think had a lot to do with his shyness and the stutter that plagued him his entire life. Mum, on the other hand, would say what had to be said, straight and to the point. She would rip a grown man to pieces with her tongue and wit. Integrity, truth and courage are her codes of honour. She stepped into the middle of brawls without fear and stood up to men who beat their wives, tearing them apart with a tirade of abuse, giving them a pedigreed reading of what a *real man* should be.

My mother has a great passion for the truth. She was instrumental in lobbying the government to have Aboriginal women recognised as wage earners in the NT Pastoral Award and though the wages were minuscule, it was a step towards equality and recognition for all women in the bush.

When Mum and Bill Tapp received an invitation to dine with the Queen on the *Queen Mary* when it docked in Darwin in the 1970s, Mum said it 'wasn't really her thing' and declined the invitation. She would much rather dine around a camp fire with ordinary people.

———

Whilst we ran wild and were adept at surviving in the harshest of conditions, it was a dangerous life for all who lived there. My little brother Joe, aged about ten at the time, ended up in hospital after going for a drive in the back tray of the ute to check fences in the wet season. The kids loved going for a drive at any time for any reason, and it was fun in the wet season when you hit bog holes and the red mud flew over the roof and splattered in your face, or the car skidded back and forth on the road.

On this occasion Clifford Cummings was driving the car with about six little kids sitting on the back, laughing and skylarking, when the car slid into the wire fence, catching Joe's arm that was hanging over the edge. He screamed as the steel fence picket gouged out a large piece of flesh at the elbow and severed the artery in his left arm. The car came to a screeching halt and they wrapped the wound tightly in a sweat-covered shirt and sped back to the station.

The doctor was called and Joe was given a large pannikin of rum to dull the pain while Mum awaited the arrival of the Flying Doctor an hour or so later.

On arrival in Katherine after vomiting up the rum on the plane, Joe had his wound stitched by Dr Scattini, who also applied a minor skin graft. A few days later when Joe's arm was put under a ray lamp to dry the infection, he suffered third-degree burns. This meant the wound had to first heal and then another skin graft had to be done with skin from the top of his thigh. Joe spent almost three months in hospital. Our Aunty Jan was a nursing sister at the hospital and looked after him. Joe says that he thinks everyone forgot he was there, as he never got a visit from our parents or any of the staff in that time. The nurses entertained him and he fattened up on the 'flash' food served up by the hospital. Soups, chicken, fresh vegetables, ice cream, 'town bread' and butter replaced the diet of beef and vegetable three times a day, seven days a week. Eventually he was picked up by the truck driver and returned home to Killarney.

Life certainly could be precarious for the kids of Killarney. One school holiday Bill Tapp asked Billy to climb up the radio telephone tower and check if there were broken wires, as the phone wasn't working and the galahs had a tendency to get into the plastic-coated wire and chew at them. Billy was about fourteen years of age, nimble and a lightweight.

We were all standing under the thin tower swaying in the wind as Billy reached the top and let out a scream. He had reached up and grabbed hold of the power line that had been stripped by the cockies. Mum was yelling at Bill Tapp, I was watching in terror and Clifford Cummings started to climb the tower when Billy managed to pull himself free from the electrical current. Billy shakily descended to earth to reveal that the wire had seared a cut right to the bone. He didn't come off too much the worse for wear in the end, and though it could have had a tragic ending, he was happy to retell the story and show the evidence of the blackened skin seared on his forefinger.

We had to contend with wild bulls, floods and bush-fires, not to mention the creepy-crawlies. One of the world's deadliest and most dangerous snakes, the king brown, scorpions and redback spiders also lurked around our home. We had many encounters with king browns getting into buildings, gardens, woodheaps, the chook house, under saddles and feed bags, and on one occasion slithering into the office under the feet of my mother and the cook. The cook and Mum flew up onto the chairs, screaming for someone to come and get the snake. The distress call was answered by Ivan Woods, the daredevil snake-catcher, who managed to hold the snake's head down with a long stick, while grabbing it by the tail and yanking it out the door, swinging it around his head to slam it on the ground and kill it. The snake was so big and heavy he let it go in mid air and it went flying, turning around and around for what seemed like forever. We all took off in every direction as it hurtled back to earth. The snake landed and was stunned long enough for Ivan to finish it off with a shovel. It was over three metres long.

Redback spiders, centipedes and scorpions could be found under beds, in boxes, under chairs and in the toilet. One New Year's Day we were all at the men's kitchen having lunch when my then three-year-old sister Caroline was bitten by a redback when she put her foot into an old boot. She was screaming in agony and I hurled her onto my hip and raced down to our house, about 500 metres through the mud. We called the doctor on the radio telephone but there was nothing else we could do as the roads to town were cut. The doctor said the most important thing was to not let her fall asleep. We did not have any major painkillers in the medicine kit suitable for a child so we just had to sit it out and hope she wouldn't die. The doctor called back every half an hour to get an update and to talk us through the incident. Caroline must have been a tough little thing because after hours of crying and a very swollen red knee where you could see the red line of the poisoned vein travelling up her little leg, the pain began to ease and we let her go to bed. She was very sick for a few days but made it through. It is awful to feel so helpless, to be unable to do anything to ease the pain, and it was very scary in those first few hours.

My mother was bitten by a scorpion on her foot which swelled to twice its size. A scorpion bite is incredibly painful; the pain lasts for days, and can recur for months. The head stockman Sandy Shaw, a big man, was also bitten by a redback when he put a shirt on and the spider was inside the shirt. It bit him on the chest and the bite left him prostrate in bed for about three days, moaning and drifting in and out of sleep with the pain.

Along with these deadly creatures, there were plenty of mosquitoes, bees, hornets, cattle ticks, bull ants and other insects with painful stings that were part of our daily life.

Mum was the doctor and the counsellor on the station. She defused family arguments and provided a shoulder to cry on for those who were suffering from isolation, domestic violence, depression and alcoholism. She organised the Flying Doctor visits and made sure that everyone turned up to get their treatment and medications for illnesses that ranged from children's immunisations, bung eyes, boils, infected sores and pre- and post-natal check-ups to leprosy, tuberculosis and herpes.

The travelling outback nursing sisters also covered the region, carrying out preventative health services to support the doctor visits. The sisters were based at Wave Hill Station, 300 kilometres west of Killarney, and they travelled on bush tracks, changing tyres and digging themselves out of bogs. They came through Killarney about six times a year and set up their clinic on the back verandah of our house. They followed up on immunisations, weighed babies, looked after cuts and broken bones and provided much-needed female contact for many station women. One of our favourites was Sister Eileen Jones, the leprosy sister, whose area covered the whole of the north end of the Northern Territory. Sister Eileen had a leg calliper – its necessity, I assume, caused by polio – and she was strong, bossy and resourceful. Sister Eileen travelled across the top end of the Northern Territory treating people with leprosy, documenting and recording the control of the disease and any new cases. In addition, and more importantly for us kids, Sister Eileen always brought black cat lollies and took lots of photos of us.

In the early years, a tuberculosis X-ray bus parked at the Killarney turn-off so all the adults from the surrounding properties could drive in to have chest X-rays. Dr Fred Hollows and his young wife, Gabi, often came to Killarney researching and treating Aboriginal people for the eye disease trachoma. I remember Gabi so clearly because she was such a beautiful girl. Dr Fred was memorable too, for his distinctive voice and laugh.

As the station developed and the roads improved, around the time I was in boarding school, more people travelled through the bush. There was a continuous procession of cattle buyers and bank managers, government departmental staff, and friends and relatives from town, all needing a meal, a bed and a few drinks. There were also the road-trains coming and going, delivering cattle to the newly built Katherine meatworks.

This constant stream of people meant that there were loads of sheets and towels to be washed, rooms to be cleaned and meals to be cooked by Mum and the domestic staff. Mum entertained bank managers, Elders GM managers, politicians and neighbouring station owners at 'the big house', while we kids ate most of the time at 'the kitchen' with the staff, and we much preferred to do that than be at home because it was much more fun talking about the cattle and horses and acting all grown up with the Killarney family.

Life might have been hard but Mum always managed to make it fun in the simplest way. She made sure everyone on the station had a birthday cake and she bought new clothes, powders and perfumes for the women and children, including her own, through mail-order catalogues. We had dress-up parties on the front verandah and everyone dressed as a cowboy, an Indian or a Mexican. There were no fairy or Cinderella dresses in our dress-up box and our outfits were easily converted from everyday wardrobes with the addition of a coloured blanket thrown over shoulders, a black moustache drawn on with a pen, or a hessian bag cut up for an Indian suit and some cockatoo feathers tied into a hat band.

Mum learnt to drive a vehicle after I did. She is a terrible driver. I would think she was the only station owner's wife in Australia whose car was a battered short wheelbase Toyota covered in stickers that read, 'Sex Appeal – Give Generously' and 'A Million Drunks Can't be Wrong' in among the 'Celebrating 10 Years of NT Self Government' and 'No Nuclear Waste Dumps in the NT'.

She loved to take all of us kids, black and white, for wheelies up the flat in her Toyota. With the canvas walls of the vehicle flapping in the wind, Mum would put her foot down and take us speeding to the 'one-mile gate'. We would all be hanging out the sides egging her on, until she hit the brakes and we came to a screeching halt in a long skid, laughing and terrified all at once of her newfound bravery. Sometimes, and depending on how much she scared herself, she would do it again. We loved every minute of it. On other occasions, Mum would take us for an evening drive out to one of the bores, singing Patsy Cline, The Platters, Jim Reeves, Charley Pride and Slim Dusty at the top of our voices as we went. Mum loves to sing; she has a great singing voice and loves Patsy Cline in particular. We knew all the songs off by heart and everyone got a chance to do a little solo of their favourite verse.

When the Patsy Cline records came out, this was a sure sign that there was a big house clean going on. Patsy and Mum bellowed 'Walking After Midnight' while Mum furiously, and with great delight, sprayed Baygon into every nook and cranny to kill the seemingly millions of cockroaches that loved the cool edges of the house foundations and lived in the drains and under the sink. She would croon away to 'Crazy' while splashing Ajax cleaning powder into sinks and baths and benches, wet tea towels over her shoulder, wielding a feather duster and cobweb broom. All the while, she would be singing and throwing out directives to me and the Aboriginal women to, 'wipe harder, don't miss that corner, use the dustpan and brush, and mop that bit of water up'. There was always plenty of cleaning to be done at Killarney so there was a lot of music and loud singing. We called Mum 'The Queen of Clean'.

It was many years before Mum built up enough courage to drive to town, and then she would convince herself that if she stopped anywhere, an axe murderer or serial killer would jump out from the bushes and slaughter us all, which meant we were not allowed to stop, even for a quick wee. There would be no point looking for the good old Territory helping hand if you were broken down by the side of the road and June Tapp went hurtling past, because she would not stop for any vehicle, in case they were murderers. She would say, 'Sing louder and don't look at them so they don't think we have seen them, just in case they are murderers,' as we sped past them with a tail of red dust, stones flying. 'Sing louder!' As the vehicle went out of sight in the rear-vision mirror, she would exhale a big sigh of relief, as if to indicate we had made a lucky escape and had survived almost being murdered.

There was one bridge on the 270-kilometre drive to town, located at the King River, 30 kilometres from Katherine, and Mum would not drive over that bridge. Despite the fact that large road-trains full of cattle drove over it, Mum would not drive across it because she said it was too narrow and her little short wheelbase Toyota might fall off! Eventually she overcame that fear and was able to drive herself to town.

Nothing can compare to the highs and the happiness of being out in the country that was your soul at sundown, with the people you loved and trusted the most in the world. We didn't need Luna Park or Kentucky Fried Chicken. We were happy, happy, happy where we were, in our own place and time. And my mother always had time to laugh and play.

Mum instilled in us a sense of appreciation of our surroundings because she loved them herself. She was interested in the trees and the plants and she liked learning about the Aboriginal people. Mum was always interested in knowing more than what was on the surface and the characters that came through Killarney certainly provided plenty of good fodder for this.

It is easy to put up with hardships if you only have to care for yourself but most women of the outback had not only to care for their husbands and children but also the station staff. The boundaries of work were very clear and stringent for the men and, though they worked physically hard and long hours, they always came home to a meal, a bed and clean clothes no matter how basic they were. For many outback women, just being pregnant and living under a bough shed would be hard enough, and yet they did everything to make life more comfortable and homely for those around them, always putting others first. Just as my mum did.

Many of the Aboriginal women on the station became part of our extended family at a time when they were not recognised as citizens of Australia and did not receive a financial reward for their work. The women mostly worked for tobacco, tea, flour, sugar, lengths of fabric and basic bedding. Aboriginal women did not have voting or drinking rights and there is very little written about them in the history books other than of their being a convenient comfort for white men, who left them with mixed-race children, no financial support nor acknowledgement that the children even existed. Many of these women eventually lost their children to welfare officers.

My mother looked after the health of the Aboriginal women on Killarney and ensured the children all attended school along with us. When Daisy and Dora retired, they were replaced by younger women who came to work on the station. Nancy Holtze arrived at Killarney with her husband, Jimmy Kelly, who was a horse tailor. She brought her three young daughters, Noreen, May and Irene (the little girl who was to tragically accidentally shoot her cousin), with her and they attended the little one-teacher school, which had been taken over by the NT Education Department, who supplied a qualified teacher and a set curriculum. Nancy worked in the house six days a week. She swept, mopped and made beds in the morning and went home for the afternoon, returning at 5 p.m. to help get the kids bathed and to take the washing off the line.

Nancy was always neat and well dressed, though she did like her beer. In the early days, Aboriginal people were not allowed to drink and when they were granted the right in 1967, very few Aboriginal women drank. Old Nancy was the first Aboriginal woman on the station allowed to have one beer a night. The men were allowed two beers a night and three on Saturdays. The beers were booked up on their tabs at the store and deducted from their wages along with tobacco, washing powder, soap and personal goods at the end of the month. Later on, soft drink was sold at the store. The young men and women were not encouraged to drink alcohol. None of the women smoked, other than my mother, who was a chain smoker; however, most of them chewed black tobacco, wedges of compressed tobacco leaves that they bit off in chunks, chewed down and rolled in ashes from the fire. The layer of ash held the tobacco in a tight wad and provided a filter that stopped the tobacco juice leaking out too quickly. They carried this wad between cheek and gum until the taste was depleted and it was replaced with a new one. The practice was just as addictive as smoking.

Nancy's daughter Noreen had her first baby with Ronnie Blitner, a ringer, at the age of fifteen. The baby was delivered by the Welsh motor mechanic Taffy Williams at Chinaman Creek, just out of Katherine. It was decided that, as he had delivered his own first baby, he was the most experienced person to cope with the emergency of delivering of a baby if needed – not thinking for a moment that this would actually happen before arriving at the hospital, as Noreen was so young. He delivered a healthy baby girl, Maureen, on the side of the highway in the middle of the night.

When the building boom was on at Killarney, new tin houses with louvres and a big breezeway between two family rooms were built for the Aboriginal families. They had electric lights, ceiling fans and cement floors, but that was it. A community shower, toilets and laundry stood as a separate building among the houses. There was only cold running water. Mum planted trees and lawns and, about once a month, she would do a run around the camp in her short wheelbase Toyota with all the kids piled into the back. The kids had to hop off and pick up all the rubbish. It was the women's responsibility to rake up, water the trees and clean the toilets and showers.

The Aboriginal women were an integral part of the function of the station and while many of the jobs would be considered menial, as I talk now to my Aboriginal friends from those years, I realise that everyone felt valued because each person was important to the functioning of our community. Whether they were raking the leaves or scraping the hair off the bull hide ropes, mustering or cooking, everyone had something to do.

Dottie Maroney arrived at Killarney as a lone mother looking for work to keep herself. She had a number of young children who had been taken by Welfare after her husband abandoned her. Dottie lived with her partner, Paddy Bennett, and everyone loved her. She was a little lady and despite the fact that she had lost her children to the Welfare she was always smiling and happy, immaculately dressed, her curly hair pulled back neatly with a coloured comb to hold it in place. Following the departure of old Nancy Holtze to an aged care facility in Katherine, Dottie took over as the senior house help. Dottie and Paddy were like parents to the younger kids in our family, particularly Daniel, who was born in 1971. They treated him like their own son. Daniel often slept at the camp with them. Dottie washed and folded the younger boys' clothes into neat piles in the cupboards and made beds to perfection. She did the washing up, dusted, swept and mopped through our large house. Dottie liked her beer and even after one too many was always ladylike. Dottie had accumulated a nice wardrobe of dresses thanks to Mum's tendency to get generous when she was having a drink – she gave a number of her designer dresses to Dottie. After seeing Dottie arrive at work one morning in a blue floral chiffon dress that Bill Tapp had bought her in Sydney, Mum said to her, and everyone else, 'Anything I give away after three drinks has to be given back to me in the morning.'

Ivy Bennett and her husband, Mickey, arrived at Killarney in 1970 with their three young children, Margaret, Michelle and Michael. Ivy was quiet and did not talk much. She was older than most of the other women on the station and her handsome husband, Mickey, was quite a bit younger than her. Her children were the apple of her eye. They were always beautifully dressed, their hair slick and bodies gleaming with the hair oil she rubbed on them. They were all shy like their mother. Mickey Bennett, a Wardaman man, replaced Sandy Shaw as the head stockman, and Ivy cooked in the men's kitchen. She baked ten double loaves of fresh bread every day along with cooking large black pots of steaming stews, curries and buckets of fresh corned beef. She would roast massive shoulder blades and topside in the outside wood stoves with crispy pumpkin, potatoes and onions. She made brownies and big pots of sweet yellow custard to go with the tinned peaches and pears.

She was a large woman and no one thought anything of her big stomach until one day one of the Aboriginal women told Mum that Ivy had had a baby in the night and that it had died. By the time Mum went to see her, Ivy had sewn the well-developed dead baby into a calico sugar bag and was wrapping it up to be buried. No one knew quite knew where the baby was buried and no one considered it their business to interfere with her way of doing what she had to do. Certainly the police weren't called – those sorts of things weren't documented if they happened in the bush.

Ena Holtze came to Killarney in 1968 to be with her mother, Nancy, and her younger sisters. Ena had a young son, Mervyn, and she worked the men's kitchen, washing up and cooking for many years. She went on to marry Kenny Wesley, the deaf fencer and family friend who started out with Bill Tapp when he was sixteen years old, droving the horses up to Montejinni Station. Ena and Kenny were a happy couple, and they had three girls, Dorcas, Carol and Sharon.

Ena's older sister Marie arrived a few years later and worked in the big house. She was tall and good looking, well spoken and had a great sense of humour. She had left her children at Barunga with her husband, Andy

Andrews. Sadly, she died of cervical cancer in the prime of her life. At her funeral they played her favourite song, 'Single Girl' by Sandy Posey. She was proud of being a strong single woman who could work, earn her own money and look after herself at a time when Aboriginal women were expected to play very strict roles as mothers and providers and it was almost impossible to survive without the support of a man.

Chapter 14

OLD MICKO

I AM NOT SURE HOW OLD MICKO CAME TO BE IN THE Northern Territory but he ended up at Killarney the way most of our employees did: falling out of the truck drunk, after being offered a job by the driver who was sent to town to pick up employees and the station stores. The driver usually did a reconnaissance of the local pub a few hours before leaving town, offering the patrons a job. Stockmen, cooks, fencers, bore runners, all sorts moved through our ever-revolving door. The ones who took up the offer were generally broke, with only the clothes on their backs and in need of a decent feed, a good dry-out and somewhere to live for a while to escape from the alcohol.

Bush cooks are strange characters with wild reputations for being bad-tempered foul-mouthed alcoholics. Cooking is a thankless job: hot and tedious, with long days that begin before the sun rises and finish long after it sets.

Whatever the circumstances of Old Micko's arrival – and we had had our share of strange cooks over the years, some who could cook and those who just said they could – we were blessed the day Old Micko fell out of that truck and into our lives in 1969. He was one of the best things to happen to us. Micko was a little man, thin and wiry, about five foot one; he had been a sapper in the 6th Division of the Australian Army that fought in the Owen Stanley Ranges in Papua New Guinea as well as in the Middle East at Benghazi and Tobruk and the siege of Badia in Egypt. Micko had the tips of the fingers missing on one hand. Whenever I asked what happened to his fingers he would answer, 'I kept the grenade and threw the pin away.'

Micko's entire wardrobe consisted of white Bonds singlets, khaki short shorts and a little towelling tennis hat to cover his balding head. His shoe wardrobe was a range of differently sized rubber thongs. He collected any stray thongs that were left lying around and if they were too big he would cut a piece off the back to make them fit his size five feet. He always had a Vegemite glass or pannikin of black tea in his hand, which we eventually figured out to be alcohol-based vanilla essence diluted in water. Micko made beautiful cakes and desserts out of virtually nothing, though he always insisted that vanilla essence was an essential ingredient. Mum eventually put two and two together when there was an order for a dozen large bottles of vanilla essence every time the truck went to town. She figured that the amount of vanilla essence being consumed was at least ten times the amount required for a month of cake making and began to wonder where it was going. I don't think she rationed the vanilla essence order too much after this discovery, though, so there was room for Micko to have the odd little tipple. Either that or the measurement for the cakes may have been diluted a little.

Micko was a placid, kind-hearted man who did not have the legendary bad temper of most bush cooks. Maybe it had something to do with the vanilla essence! He was also the most amazing cook and gardener. Though well into his fifties when he first came to live with us, he set up a large half-acre vegetable garden with rows of elegant nodding sunflowers around the perimeter. We ate thick yellow corn on the cob and bright orange carrots, fresh tomatoes, juicy green beans and bowls of fresh peas. We gave away boxes of excess vegetables to the stock inspectors, pilots and truckies. Micko filled large coffee jars with pickled beetroots, chillies and chutneys, and took care of more than a hundred chooks, feeding them the garden and kitchen scraps and collecting the eggs. All this, and feeding up to forty people three big meals and two smokos a day.

In the early days he achieved all of this out of an incredibly hot kitchen with a huge wood-fired stove, until a new brick kitchen with air conditioning and big stainless steel gas stoves was built. Micko helped with the design of the new kitchen in 1970 and it was his pride and joy to have one of the most modern station kitchens in the Northern Territory, with large stainless steel stoves and sinks big enough to swim in.

He made sixteen double loaves of fresh fluffy bread with golden crusts every day, getting up at four in the morning to start the dough. He cooked massive trays of crispy baked potatoes, pumpkin and onion to accompany big slabs of roast beef with jugs of steaming homemade gravy. Big pots boiled endlessly on the top of the stove filled with corned beef and large yellow flaps of fat rendering down into dripping.

The radio stayed on all day and night in the kitchen. Micko was a Labor man at a time when Labor was a dirty word in the Territory and very few people owned up to being a Labor voter. He said he had voted Labor all his life until the local conservative Member for Victoria River came through and gave him a bottle of rum. He voted Liberal that year.

Old Micko only left the station once a year, for his wet season bender in town, where he stayed at the Riverview Motel. There he drank his annual pay cheque and returned home with the clothes he stood up – or, should I say, fell over – in. He would be dumped at his room until he finally ventured out a few days later as the shakes subsided, and he could stand on his rickety legs to return to work.

Our large family became his. Though he spoke regularly about his family, only once in the twenty or so years did he venture south when my mother convinced him that he should go and see his only surviving brother on the Sunshine Coast. He arrived back at Killarney six weeks later, very drunk, in a little battered blue Holden Torana that he had bought and conned a couple of mates into driving back to the Territory because he had had enough of the south. Micko had never learnt to drive and asked me to teach him when I was about fourteen years old. After a few bunny hops up and down the flat, he decided driving was not for him and he was too old to learn, so he gave the car away.

When Micko cooked for Christmas, we ate like royalty. He prepared every morsel of food lovingly and with pride. He shook off compliments with the air of one who knew there was no better than him. Christmas sent Micko into rapture, because he had access to a wide range of special ingredients, including an extra supply of vanilla essence, whisky, port and sherry for the puddings and cakes. He always ordered double amounts of alcohol, of course, to ensure there was a cup for the pudding and a cup for the creator.

The kitchen would be a production line of fruitcakes, mince pies, coconut ice, peanut brittle, chocolate fudge, marshmallows and homemade sauces and gravies. We loved it, as he would let us lick the bowls clean and test the goodies. The ham was wrapped and cured in the cold room and large headless turkeys lined up all white and prickly waiting for their turn in the oven. The fruits – cherries, plums, apricots, peaches and pears – all looked too good to eat. The Aboriginal children eyed the fruits suspiciously and were often too frightened to taste them as they had never seen them before.

Micko was at his best at Christmas, staggering from his room in the men's quarters through the thick black mud, carrying his thongs and a green can. On one particular night, when we were all partying on well into the early hours of the morning, a weak little voice came through the darkness and pelting rain during a lull in the music and the drunken rabble.

'Help, mate! Help, mate!'

Micko had fallen into the metre-deep gutter that was cut in with the grader between the men's quarters and kitchen. In the wet season it formed a mini raging river that steered the torrential water past the buildings and out into the paddock. The gutter had a couple of planks across to form a little bridge. Micko had missed the bridge on his way home and was legs up, hands flailing in the air, one holding his can of beer and packet of cigarettes, the dirty water rushing over him. He would surely have drowned if we hadn't heard him.The wet season was a challenge for everyone, with the roads cut off for months on end, and it was too hot and wet to grow vegetables. With Christmas over, our diet would revert to stringy dried bits of corned beef, pumpkin, potatoes and onions for breakfast, lunch and dinner; baked, stewed and boiled, anything for a little variety in presentation of the same monotonous ingredients. The bread was made out of stale weevilly flour and when the yeast ran out, crusty dampers were baked in the camp ovens.

Micko was a master of making mouth-watering meals out of nothing. A few egg whites and sugar beaten for half an hour produced beautiful meringues; sugar and water made tooth-cracking toffees. An old slab of beef rubbed with a few dried herbs, Worcestershire sauce and cooked with vegies in the camp oven brimming with fat became a tasty, belly-filling meal.

Micko would save his cigarette butts for when the store ran out of tobacco. He would shake the last few stale leaves from several black butts into a bowl and roll them in a fresh cigarette paper to make up another cigarette. His eyes would glaze over with relief as the nicotine hit his lungs.

Running out of tobacco and alcohol could shake the soul of the hardiest bushman and, combined with the weather, send tempers to boiling. Some desperados were known to filter car brake fluid through large slabs of bread and drink the clear liquid that came out the bottom, which supposedly had alcohol in it. Whether it was all in the imagination or very real alcohol I am not sure, but it seemed to calm nerves and give them a high. Micko sensibly had a spare bottle of vanilla essence or alcohol-based cough mixture hidden away to control the shakes.

I often wondered in later years why making alcohol never became a wet season industry, and put it down to the lack of fruit and vegetables, but I am sure there must have been lots of bush tucker that could have been brewed into a nice alcoholic drink to keep the shakes away if anyone had ever thought of it.

Micko was always good for a laugh as he perched on his flour drum, waving his beer can around, cigarette hanging out the side of his mouth and Coke bottle glasses perched crookedly on his nose, reciting dirty ditties learnt in the Far East. He never complained when he woke up in the morning to find we had given him a pudding bowl haircut.

'There's only a week between a good haircut and a bad haircut,' he would say as he pulled his little blue towelling hat over his head. I often used to think that if he just donned a brown sugar sack he could enter a seminary with Friar Tuck. Poor Old Micko, we would do mean things to him, like hide his tobacco and grog, but he never really got upset. However, if he swore, you knew that he was angry and the joke was over.

As he got older, Micko retired from the cooking and just maintained the vegetable garden and the chooks, helping with bread making and creating beautifully decorated birthday cakes. Absolutely everyone got a special birthday cake with candles.

At this time he also bought himself a retirement caravan and moved out of the single room in the men's quarters that he had lived in for years. The caravan was perched out on the flat among the rocks but gave him the independence of cooking for himself and allowed him to set up his huge reel-to-reel tape player to boom out country music. We had some great parties there. The caravan came to a sad end when he had one drink too many and burnt it to the ground.

Old Micko finally retired to the Red Cross home in Katherine, where he lived out his last days. He always had a cheery 'g'day, mate' for everyone, no matter how sick he was. He never wanted anyone to fuss over him. As far as anyone knows, he never married nor had a partner.

Old Micko, digger and chef extraordinaire, was one of those people who rolled into our lives and made it richer. He gave us plenty of laughs and plenty of good tucker and never made an enemy. He is buried with many of his alcoholic bush mates, including Pat and Tom Quirk, at the Katherine Cemetery.

———

Our lives were mostly happy, but of course there were times of contention and dissension, family fallouts, arguments and the occasional firing of a gun in anger. More often than not, the arguments were the result of excess consumption of alcohol.

During the wet season some of the regulars would go away for a couple of months, bingeing in town. When they returned, at the end of the Wet, they had to be 'brought down' gently. This involved allowing the person to sleep all day and being doled out a pannikin of rum at lunchtime and a couple of beers in the evening for the first few days, while the cook served up good solid stews and mashed potato to line the stomach. Most often, stockmen arrived back on the station with only the clothes they stood up in, so Mum would have to do big orders for new clothing, bedding, swags and boots, which were debited against their wages.

We had a family with four little children come from Queensland to work for us. The father, John, was a likeable man and a very good stockman, but he was a sad and chronic alcoholic. On one occasion when he broke his arm, my cousin Robyn and I, both aged eighteen, drove him the 270 kilometres to town to have the arm X-rayed and plastered. We dropped him at the hospital and by the time we went to pick him up an hour or so later, he had caught a taxi to the pub. Robyn and I had a number of jobs to do, picking up stores and the mail, so when we found him he was almost catatonic. Lucky for us there were only two pubs in Katherine, so he was easy to find.

I rang home and asked Bill Tapp what we should do. Should we wait till he sobered up or come home without him? Bill Tapp said, 'Just get in him in the car and come straight home.'

We conned John to get into the car with the purchase of a bottle of rum and went roaring out of town in a little short wheelbase Toyota with no sides.

About 20 kilometres out of town, John, perched on top of the stores and mailbag, came alive and starting abusing us, waving his bottle of rum around and telling us to turn around and go back to town. He started to climb out the side as we were hurtling down the road, hanging his legs over and screaming, 'If you don't turn around I am going to jump out.'

We were scared that he would jump so we slowed down in the hope that if he did, he would not kill himself. We knew that if we stopped, we would not get him back into the vehicle. We discussed whether we should leave him there, go on to home, or take him back to town. We decided to keep driving and told him to shut up and enjoy his bottle of rum. He finally passed out for the rest of the journey, plaster intact around his broken arm.

One evening, just as we were sitting down to dinner, we were jolted by a massive gunshot resounding across the station. Everyone bolted for cover. The Aboriginal people, who always ate outside in family groups, fled into the kitchen, the women and children screaming, while the stockmen hid behind doors and buildings.

We knew where the shot had come from, because John had been on a bender.

My mother pushed newcomer Shaun Coutts, who had only been on the station for about two weeks, out the door and said, 'Quick, you go and get the gun off him.'

Shaun crept around the building towards the house as though he was in a cowboy movie, only to see the mother and her four children lying terrified in a shallow gutter about fifty metres from the house. John was waving a .303 around drunkenly in the dark. Shaun yelled at John to put the gun down, talking and coaxing him, and finally John let Shaun take the gun from him.

After he disarmed John, Shaun removed the bullets from the chamber and the family returned to the house, and the rest of us went back to dinner. A few days later, John came out of the house, shaky and a little coy, and we knew it would not be long before there was another incident.

We would say to Bill Tapp, 'Why don't you sack him?' but Bill Tapp was adamant that while these were not ideal situations, at least the mother had a home and food for her family and the children a school to go to. They stayed on for about three years after the .303 incident. Things did not improve and finally Bill Tapp had to sack John; luckily, the family were able to go to their family-owned property in the Territory where the children and mother had some security, a home and schooling.

John's wife never gave up on him even though his alcoholism got worse. One day, he was returning to the station from a drinking binge in town. He stopped the vehicle and passed out under a tree, where he choked on his own vomit and died beside his car.

—

Our world was certainly a microcosm of global society. We had an Irish painter, Paddy, who lived with us for many years, painting all the new buildings, cattle yards and gates. He only ever wore 'painter whites', which were shorts and T-shirts, and he treated his paintbrushes and equipment like the crown jewels. He did not like us kids and would always tell us to 'Fook off, you little coonts.' The more we teased, the more he swore and the more we laughed at his funny accent.

Paddy would go on the customary wet season bender and spend all his savings. One year he returned with a tiny white caravan and a lovely Aboriginal woman called Marjorie, who came from Western Australia. Other than the odd argument, they kept to themselves and seemed to live happily in their van parked out on the black soil flat under a shadeless tree. Every now and then, they would go on a bender together.

On one occasion, Marjorie, who could not drive, jumped into Paddy's white ute full of equipment and went screaming around the flat, kangaroo hopping, skidding and fishtailing until she came to a screeching halt just metres away from the men's kitchen door. She jumped out in a rage, picked up a big rock and smashed two of the windows in the guest dining room, all the while screaming and cursing everyone and everything. As was the norm at Killarney, Marjorie was eventually placated and sent home, and the glass windows replaced.

In happier times, Paddy bought Marjorie nice clothes and, after attending the local Show, gave her a little box full of bright plastic necklaces, bangles and rings that she loved. When they had an argument, Paddy would confiscate all Marjorie's jewellery. She would wail, 'That Paddy, he is no good – he stole all my jewels! Can you make Paddy give my jewels back to me please?' He would return the jewels, and they lived happily together until the next drinking spree.

One evening in the wet season, three of my young brothers were sent out in an open-top bull catcher, which had a gun mounted on the dash in a holster, to pick up the truck driver who had bogged a truck full of drum diesel and food stores, approximately 30 kilometres from the station. They were to bring the driver home for the night and return in the morning to pull the truck out.

The driver had consumed a large amount of alcohol on his 250-kilometre trip home and went into a rage when the boys argued over whose turn it was to open the gate. The man drew the gun on them and waved them all out of the vehicle, then sped off into the night, leaving them stranded in the dark. The boys were terrified – Billy was the oldest, at sixteen – and they started to walk home on the wet season night, lightning flashing all around them.

The man returned about half an hour later and called out to them, 'Don't be silly now – come on out.' He had obviously worked out even in his drunken rage that there was going to be questions asked if he arrived home in the bull catcher without the boss's three sons.

When the man stopped and got out of the car to plead with them to get back in, Billy wrestled the gun from him and told him to get in and shut up; the man obeyed and they drove home, the man now subdued in his alcoholic stupor.

As we discuss these incidents as grownups, my siblings and I marvel at the things that we put up with and at the acceptance of all these strange, damaged characters. We also marvel that all ten of us survived and agree that what doesn't kill you only makes you stronger.

Chapter 15

CRACKS IN THE HIDE

CENTRE STAGE TO ALL THIS DYSFUNCTION WERE MY loving, warring parents.

As the prosperity of the property grew, so did my parents' propensity for overindulgence in all the good things of life. It was Bill Tapp, in particular, who went on spending sprees, staying at five-star hotels and buying televisions, cameras, videos, high-priced stallions, bulls, trucks and equipment. Mum rarely went away because she didn't like flying and there were too many kids to look after, and certainly too many to take away on a family holiday. Bill Tapp's drinking increased over time and then Mum started to drink as well. I noticed this when I was home from boarding school in the early 1970s. Mum was a binge drinker rather than a regular drinker, but she seemed to be bingeing quite a lot. The raging, screaming arguments intensified and became more physical, with them both lashing out at each other. I would pull the pillow over my head and pretend nothing was happening. Mum spent nights locking herself in the guest quarters about 200 metres away from our house. During the day, she searched for stashed-away alcohol in cupboards and drawers and in the garden to prevent Bill Tapp from drinking. Many a time she stood out on the front lawn and pulled zip-top after zip-top off cartons of beer and poured them out, one by one. Over the years, she poured out or smashed hundreds of bottles of beer and Johnnie Walker whisky.

When Bill Tapp went away, they would carry on their arguments over the radio telephone. All calls were monitored by the telephonists, because they had to come on the line to ask if the caller was extending. One can only imagine how they must have felt when they had to interrupt a very loud argument well peppered with the best of swear words! The phone was located in the office, about 50 metres from our house. The screaming air-raid siren that announced a phone call would pierce through the night each time one of my parents hung up on the other and then called back.

Bill Tapp loved material things and the good life but was not prone to spending money on the house or himself. His daily dress was a pair of tattered trousers, a pair of torn desert boots with missing laces and the tongue hanging out protruding from under them. His dusty, sweat-stained shirt with a rip right down the back always had a red Elders notebook and pen in the front pocket. This uniform was topped by the well-worn ten-gallon hat that rarely left his head.

We hardly ever had hot water after the solar water system broke down while I was away at school, and Bill Tapp wouldn't pay to have it fixed. Mum was bathing little kids in the laundry tubs and washing the endless piles of filthy jeans in cold water. I don't think Bill Tapp really ever considered that this was a hardship because he didn't mind a cold shower and always had clean clothes, of course. I don't think he really ever thought about the impact of his habits and the hardship it caused the women.

Periodically, Mum would go into a rage about the leaking roof and broken-down washing machines, and the station handyman would materialise to pacify her and sort out the problems. As most were bush handymen with few carpentry or electrical skills, the problems were generally exacerbated.

While I was at boarding school Bill Tapp built a new two-room office, one for Mum and the larger one for himself. I was able to move into the old office attached to an outdoor bathroom and laundry about 50 metres from the main house. This not only helped a little in being able to remove myself from the fighting and yelling at night, but it also meant I could turn the cassette player up and sing at the top of my lungs – country music, of course. I revelled in having my own space and when my cousin Robyn came to stay in the school holidays, we could stay up all night playing the guitar and writing songs. We could also sneak out to Apartment No 5, the tin house where all the young men lived.

Following the death of Bill Tapp's mother on the Gold Coast in 1971, a truckload of beautiful furniture, crockery and paintings that included an original Albert Namatjira arrived at Killarney. After a few years in my family's possession, the delicate Queen Anne table and chairs required a polish and buff to remove stains. Tom Quirk convinced Mum that he knew how to strip and restore furniture. Mum, as always, trusted that if someone told her they had particular skills, they would deliver. No one took any notice as Tom polished and buffed the table on the front verandah and when Mum had a look at the shiny restored table she was horrified to see he had sanded it back and painted over it with mission brown housepaint!

Though his stutter and shyness caused him great discomfort, Bill Tapp was passionate about animal rights and the development of the NT cattle industry. The 1970s saw rapid change coming to the bush and issues such as better roads, land rights, bovine tuberculosis, foot and mouth disease, health and education were on the agenda of the Cattlemen's Association of Northern Australia, of which Bill Tapp was president. Constitutional reform and Territorians wanting more control of their land were also on the agenda.

Bill Tapp's opinions were sought on a wide range of Territory issues that affected the cattle industry, including mustering techniques, animal welfare, road and transport infrastructure, disease control, pastoral award wages and the establishment of the Katherine meatworks. As reported in the *NT News*, he told the then Minister for the Northern Territory, Kep Enderby, that 'Rural land settlement in the NT is an ad hoc, slow, piecemeal process which is effectively keeping the Territory's graziers out of the industry'.

The Aboriginal land rights movement was gaining momentum across Australia and a Federal Government report, the 1971–1974 Gibb Report, recommended that certain areas of cattle stations be given over to Aboriginal people. These recommendations resulted in heated debate and resistance from Territory cattlemen, and instigated the formation of the Equal Rights for Territorians protest group, of which my mother was an active supporter. This group was commonly called 'Rights for Whites' in an effort by the media to stir up racial tension; however, those involved always insisted that their issues were many and varied and were about allowing Territorians to make their own decisions about land tenure and legislation, as opposed to those decisions being made thousands of kilometres away in Canberra.

Many of the people involved in the Cattlemen's Association, which was one of the largest and most organised lobby groups in the NT at the time, went on to become the first members of the NT Legislative Assembly when self-government was granted on 1 July 1978. These included the Chairman of the Rights for Territorians group, Les MacFarlane, from Moroak Station south of Katherine.

Mum became the first woman to be active in the Cattlemen's Association to champion the rights of Aboriginal women, who were excluded from the NT Cattle Industry Award. She pushed to have the role of 'Domestics' awarded a legal minimum wage. Mum wrote endless letters to ministers, department heads and newspapers about the poor state and lack of equity in health, education and award wages. She told the NT News, 'There is a crying need for female domestics employed on pastoral properties to be covered by a wage award. There has been much fuss made about what men earn on stations. What about women? If they received more, then I suggest more of it would be put to good use. They [the women] are perhaps more likely to spend the money on children, etc – as opposed to themselves.'

Chapter 16

THE SCOTSMAN

I MET MY HUSBAND, SHAUN COUTTS, WHEN HE CAME TO Killarney to manage the Santa Gertrudis show cattle team. He had arrived in the Northern Territory with the baptism of a massive wet season that saw him stranded in Katherine for two weeks and staying at the newly built Corroboree Motel, managed by the outrageous and eccentric Territorian Sylvia Wolf.

A reserved Scotsman who had left his home in Crieff as a seventeen-year-old with a boatload of Black Angus Bulls being exported to New Zealand in 1964, Shaun intended to stay for a year and return home. But the man his father had organised to meet him off the boat and give him a job never arrived at the port to pick him up, so Shaun had no choice but to find accommodation and a job. Before he knew it, he had spent seven years in New Zealand becoming an accomplished farmer. Having taught himself to play the piano accordion on the six-week boat trip to New Zealand, he played with the Hamilton County Bluegrass Band, doing gigs all over the North and South Islands.

Brought up in a very strict Presbyterian household with a minister grandfather and a lay minister father, Shaun took his religion seriously and decided to take up an offer to work at the Wayside Chapel in Sydney with the outspoken and evangelical Reverend Ted Noffs. Within weeks, Shaun decided this was not his scene and found a job working as a jackaroo on Brewon Station near Walgett in New South Wales. A short time after arriving there, he had a horse fall and broke his back, landing him in Royal North Shore Hospital in Sydney for nine months.

Shaun did not know anyone in Sydney. His father, Ben Coutts, made contact with an Australian man, Frank Gardiner, whom he had met during the war, and asked him to look after his son. The Gardiner family took Shaun in as one of their own, regularly visiting him in hospital, providing him with a home when he left hospital and helping him to get a job. He subsequently worked on a variety of cattle properties, ending up at the Coorong in

South Australia, where he saw an advertisement in *The Land* magazine for a job on a cattle station in the Northern Territory.

Shaun met Bill Tapp in Adelaide for the interview. Bill Tapp had gone to Adelaide to meet with the senior management of Elders GM, the major financiers of Killarney, and he liked Shaun immediately, so he offered him the job of managing the show cattle and the top pay of $70 per week.

On his return from Adelaide, Bill Tapp told me that he had found me a 'tall, dark and handsome' man. I was not interested in this new tall, dark and handsome man – though I had to admit when I saw him that he was definitely as described – as I was going out with a gorgeous part-Aboriginal man called Frankie Hayes, whose brother Gary had worked for us for a number of years. Frankie and I were passionately in love and did everything together. We both loved country music, writing songs, and art. We spent a lot of time planning midnight rendezvous at various spots around the station because he shared a house with five other young single men. We got to know the saddle shed and hay shed and other secret locations intimately, though years later I learnt they were not so secret, as they were the meeting places of most station lovers. Frankie and I loved to take all the kids swimming at one of the various turkey's nest dams every afternoon while the rest of the station had siesta between lunch and afternoon smoko.

Our relationship was not socially acceptable and caused some talk, but I was blissfully unaware and, typical of an eighteen-year-old, I didn't care anyway.

Eventually, Frankie moved back to town to work and we drifted apart. I moved to Katherine and lived at my grandmother's house. I washed dishes at the Transport and Works Department dining room during the day and sold beer in the Saloon Bar at the Crossways Hotel at night to save money to go to Sydney. Working in these places added to my repertoire of crazy friends and acquaintances from Killarney who were running away from family, the law, the tax office and shady deals.

Frankie was sadly killed in a domestic violence incident in the late 1980s.

Shaun would visit me when he came to town to pick up stores or drop off cattle to the meatworks; he'd stay at my grandmother's. We eventually started going out. At the end of the year, Shaun decided to go back to work at King Ranch in Bowral, New South Wales, and I went with him. My parents seemed to accept my decision and didn't try to talk me out of leaving, though Bill Tapp did his usual delaying tactics, pleading for us to stay and help out with the final muster, so that we left a month later than planned.

We drove down to Sydney in Shaun's white Ford ute with his blue heeler dog in the back. I stayed for a few weeks with Bill Tapp's old school friends David and Claire Brockhoff until I found a job and a place to live.

I worked for a very short while at the Jorg Jensen Silversmith Shop in Centrepoint before finding a full-time job in the filing section of the Department of Environment and Planning. I delivered trollies full of files around the floors, chain smoking and flirting with all the young planners and architects. Many of the workers were intrigued to know a 'real person' from the Northern Territory, part of Australia that the southern population knew very little about. The southerners all assumed we ate buffalo and lived on croc-infested rivers. They thought that Aboriginal people walked around naked, dead kangaroos hanging over their shoulders, and spears at the ready to kill any poor unsuspecting white person they came across. An older man who had worked as a town planner in the department for most of his life loved asking me about the bush, my family and the station life. He followed stories about the Land Rights movement and letters to the editor written by my mother in *The Bulletin*.

I made many friends, going to the pubs on Friday night and down to Bowral to see Shaun on the weekends. I lived in a flat in Edgecliff with a Kiwi girl and a pot-smoking Moroccan called Hassan, who never had a job but always had plenty of cash and seemed to be always busy, coming and going at all hours of the day and night. When one of his friends barged into my room one night and tried to get into my bed, I packed up and moved to a house on the North Shore. During this time two of my younger brothers, Sam and Joe, were sent to The Scots College in Bellevue Hill and Shaun and I would take them out on weekends.

Mum and Bill Tapp came to Sydney to visit us and stayed at the Cosmopolitan Hotel in Double Bay. A week into the visit, Bill Tapp went on a big drinking binge. Mum was stuck in a hotel room with him for all this time. She would not drive in Sydney and was not a very confident traveller, but she did eventually pack up and leave. I was blissfully unaware of the entire goings-on until I got a phone call at work from a very drunk and crying Bill Tapp asking if I knew where Mum was. I left work, distraught and worried and looking for Mum, who, by the time I got to the hotel, had returned.

In between all the tension, Mum took me shopping in Double Bay, buying me all the latest fashions: wedge shoes, mini and maxi dresses, hot pants, long evening dresses and lots of beads and blue eyeshadow. It was very exciting for the now streetwise bush girl who did most of her shopping at an op shop in the city.

I stayed in Sydney for about fifteen months and I returned to Killarney in 1975. My relationship with Shaun broke down because we were too far apart and I wanted to go home to the red dirt, spindly trees and my dysfunctional family, whereas Shaun didn't, and I can't blame him for that. On leaving Sydney, I made plans to return and go to New Zealand with some girlfriends at the end of the year.

I had only been back at Killarney for a few months when Shaun lost his job due to a crash in the Australian cattle industry that saw hundreds of farms and cattle stations forced into bankruptcy. Bill Tapp, having a soft spot for Shaun, invited him to return to Killarney. We casually took up the relationship again and when I returned to Sydney for the New Zealand trip at the end of the year, Shaun and I flew south together, he getting off in Adelaide, and me in Sydney, assuming that this was the end of our relationship again.

I was having a great time with my girlfriends going out on the town, including a night in Kings Cross, and was very surprised to get a phone call from Shaun a week later, asking me to pick him up from the train in Bowral, where I was staying with my girlfriend.

Shaun arrived the following cold, wet morning, twenty-four hours before I was due to leave for New Zealand. I had borrowed my friend's car to pick him up from the train station and we made small talk as we returned to her place. I was totally gobsmacked when he said he had come up to ask me to marry him! I had not got the impression that there were going to be any wedding bells between us. I went bright red and said I had to go to the toilet. When I caught my breath and got my thundering heart under control, I returned to the lounge room and said, 'Can I tell you when I get home from New Zealand?'

I was just twenty years old and Shaun was twenty-nine. I said yes – before I went to New Zealand – and then he said we would have to go to town and ring Bill Tapp from the phone box, reverse charges, so he could ask for my hand in marriage. Once he'd done so, we went to a little jewellery shop in Mittagong and bought the cheapest diamond ring we could find. By this time I felt like a real princess and the day after went to New Zealand an engaged girl, proudly flashing my little diamond.

One of the things I loved about Shaun – beside his being tall, dark and handsome – was his beautiful singing voice. My grandmother had said to me after a party at her house, where Shaun held the floor, playing his piano accordion and singing all the great old Scottish and Irish songs, 'You can't let a voice like that go, Toni. You'd better marry him and keep him in the family.'

A few years later, Shaun's good friend Ned Campagnolo in Mansfield told me that Shaun was visiting him at the time and he had said to him, 'You'd better marry that girl – she is a good sort, and you'd better get up there and put a ring on her finger before she goes to New Zealand and some young Kiwi fella snaps her up.' Forty years and the rest is history!

I returned from New Zealand and spent two weeks working on a dairy with 200 milking cows. I was well used to cattle, wild ones at that, but this was the worst job I have had in my life. Not being an early-morning person and having to get up on freezing cold mornings to milk the cows that dropped great big loads of sloppy warm manure all over the place, including on your head, was not my idea of a good job. I much preferred the wild, unpredictable cattle of Killarney. The one consolation was the jugs of beautiful fresh milk that I scooped out of the spinning stainless steel tanks and topped with a big splash of duty-free Kahlua for breakfast every morning.

I decided to buy a wedding dress before flying home. It was the wet season in the Territory and there was not a lot of choice of wedding dresses in Darwin, which was still recovering from Cyclone Tracy a year prior. I spent days walking around Sydney looking in wedding shops, trying on dresses and drooling over the huge white balloons of taffeta, satin and silk. However, as much I wanted the big fairy princess wedding, I knew that the frou-frou frocks with leg-of-mutton sleeves topped by lace veils that were the fashion were not going to suit my outback wedding.

I went back to the first dress I'd fallen in love with from my favourite designer boutique, a shop that I walked past every day on my way to work, always stopping to drool over the beautiful dresses I could never afford: The House of Merivale. The long, straight, body-hugging, backless crepe dress with lace appliqué up one side that came with a tight peplum jacket was far more elegant and suitable to the Killarney climate and my lifestyle.

I arrived home at the end of January 1976 newly engaged and went straight into a frenzy of wedding planning, a very difficult task in the middle of the wet season with the crackly radio telephone and irregular mail deliveries. I wrote for samples of fabrics for bridesmaid's dresses and stationery for the invitations. The wedding date was set for the May school holidays to ensure that my younger brothers and sisters would be home from boarding school.

Invitations were sent everywhere across Australia, to politicians, business people, all the cattle station people in the district, the employees, family and friends. My mother sent invitations to her idols of the day, including Prince Leonard and Princess Shirley of Hutt River Principality in Western Australia, whom she had never met but had written letters to. Mum was a great fan of Prince Leonard's (much to Bill Tapp's and many other people's disgust) because Prince Leonard had taken on the Australian Government and seceded from Australia to become his own country within Western Australia.

The day of the wedding arrived, frantic with food preparation, setting up tables and chairs, and the bar. Mum swept around the station greeting the guests, directing them to camping areas to set out their swags and camps. My great-grandmother had travelled up from New South Wales and we were so excited to have four generations of women together to celebrate my outback wedding. We got dressed in the guest quarters, the men in one room and the women in the other. My cousins Robyn and Vicki and sister Shing were my bridesmaids, dressed in long, blue floral dresses. My crepe dress was topped by a white floppy hat dressed with flowers from the garden. Nana and her friend Mrs Scott made a big bouquet from pink and white bougainvillea. Shaun and the groomsmen wore blue tight-fitting trousers, white shirts and blue floral ties.

The men's quarters overflowed with city women donning taffeta dresses after the 270-kilometre drive. Every available bathroom was a tumble of excited chatter, irons, hairdryers, lipstick and perfume. The men donned their suits behind cars while wives and girlfriends applied their blue eyeshadow and mascara in the rear-view mirrors.

Long tables were laid out on the back lawn and dressed with white linen tablecloths before large pots of beef stroganoff, bolognaise, pastas and steaming vegetables were added. The double-layered white wedding cake decorated with intricate handmade marzipan frangipanis glowed under the hundreds of party lights strung across the garden. The bar was set up in outdoor laundry tubs filled with ice, and Champagne glasses sparkled as the sun set in a golden glow across our wedding celebration.

We were to be married at 4.30 p.m. on the front verandah of the house, watched by 250 guests, but were told that we had to wait for half an hour as the truck with the alcohol had just arrived and they had to get the grog into the drums of ice. It was a great relief for everyone to know the beer truck had arrived at all, as the driver, Pat Quirk, was not the first person one would want to be driving a truck loaded with alcohol. The eight kegs of beer and a 100 bottles of Beenleigh Rum, Johnnie Walker Red Label Whisky and cartons of sparkling wine were swiftly unloaded. I walked up the path on Bill Tapp's arm, him dapper in long black pants, white shirt and polka-dot tie. My younger brothers and sisters and the Aboriginal children were dressed in blue jeans and white shirts, and formed a guard of honour as I walked onto the verandah. Mum leant out her bedroom window, dressed in a flowing floral dress with a large picture hat and a pair of black and hot pink candy-striped platform rubber thongs. Brother Paul from the Church of England in Katherine was there to officiate.

Earlier in the day Mum, who was disillusioned with marriage, said, 'Women don't have to marry these days; if you don't want to get married, don't worry, we can still have a big party!'

My brother Sam brought his friend Chris Atkinson from Scots College for the holidays. Chris brought his bagpipes and piped us to the wedding table to sign the marriage certificate once the ceremony was complete.

It was a chilly night and fire drums were lit in the garden to keep everyone warm during the reception. My uncle Jim was the master of ceremonies and the speeches were kept short and sweet. It was an emotional night for me, as Bill Tapp told the crowd how proud he was of me, his first-born stepdaughter. Mum, never one to take the back seat, also gave a speech and welcomed Shaun into the family. After the formalities, the ladies sat around fire drums talking and drinking tea, and the men gathered in bunches to share their stories. The younger ones danced the night away on the front verandah to a rocking four-piece band from Katherine.

As the crowd thinned, we moved into the kitchen and were playing the guitars and singing until Bill Tapp arose at 3 a.m. and kicked us out of the house so everyone could get some sleep. Shaun and I returned to the guest quarters for the night as the last of the revellers were falling into their swags, the sun rising in the east.

The next morning, Mum was up early, ringing the kitchen siren to wake everyone up. Two hundred and fifty people sat bolt upright in their swags as most had never heard such a noise. Before long the big barbecue was fired up by Goff Letts, leader of the NT Legislative Assembly, to cook the thick lumps of meat, sausages and eggs to feed the hungover guests. Large pots of tea and coffee were being laced with painkillers for the sore heads. After breakfast, as stomachs settled and headaches eased, the lids were popped off cold cans of beer and the party continued well into the evening. Bill Tapp held court and offered a twenty-dollar reward to any child who could find his false teeth. Henry the gardener had decided in his delirium to 'pull out' and took the ride-on lawnmower as his mode of transport, to ride the 40 kilometres to the Top Springs pub. He only got about 2 kilometres down the uneven rocky road when he decided that it was not a very good idea and returned.

Most of the guests had left by Monday and Shaun had to take the truck full of empty beer kegs back to town. My great-grandmother stayed for the week, as did Mum's pen pal of twenty years, an elderly lady whom she had never met until she came to the wedding.

Shaun and I moved into one of the two-bedroom houses on the station, which was a great honour for us. We set up all our beautiful wedding presents, silver trays and tea sets, dinner sets, vases, toaster and electric jug. I loved playing house and made bold black and red curtains for the windows and groovy cushion covers.

Life continued for us: big musters of cattle, drafting and branding long into the night, and road-trains of cattle leaving the station for the meatworks to pay the bills. I worked in the office, badly typing letters in which Bill Tapp asked for extensions on paying bills, and running the station store while Shaun worked with the stud cattle, sorting, taming and grooming them for the show.

———

Shaun and I settled into our little brick house with an outside toilet and bathroom, and carried on working at home for the rest of the year, but we decided that we needed to leave Killarney to gain our own identity and to save as much as possible to have a honeymoon in Scotland for me to meet the Coutts family.

In November 1976, we packed up our second-hand station wagon with all our household goods and headed off to Mansfield in Victoria, where Shaun had a job lined up with a friend. A week after we arrived, I celebrated my twenty-first birthday in a large old wooden house in Bonnie Doon with a fireplace and no furniture, watching the water skiers skimming over the sparkling waters of Lake Eildon.

The farm job fell through before we arrived, so Shaun spent the first summer clearing trees for a new ski slope at Mt Buller while I worked at the Delatite Hotel. We worked a variety of jobs and made friends through the football community and the Apex Club. Within two years, we had saved enough to take our trip overseas to meet the Scottish family. My cousin and best friend Robyn Forscutt came with us.

I found the spectacular landscape and remoteness of the Highlands not dissimilar to New Zealand, and indeed country Victoria, where we lived for four years.

I found that Shaun's family was as eccentric as mine, had many similarities and I loved them all instantly. My father-in-law, Captain Ben (John Barnaby) Coutts, was a big charismatic man, outgoing; he loved his cattle, politics, whisky and God. Ben had been wounded in the Second World War and spent twelve months in a London hospital having his face reconstructed by Sir Archibald McIndoe, a pioneering plastic surgeon who worked for the Royal Air Force during the war, treating and doing reconstructive surgery on badly burned aircrew. Shaun's father, part of the team later known as the 'guinea pigs', had lost his nose and part of his face and this was rebuilt by Sir Archibald. Ben was the Secretary of the Aberdeen Society of Scotland and had his own radio farming program for over twenty years. The Queen Mother was the Patron of the Aberdeen Angus Society and she shared a 'wee dram' with Captain Ben every year at the Royal Highland Show until his passing. Ben stood a number of times for the Scottish Liberal Party, using the slogan 'Big Ben for London'. He also wrote five books about his involvement in the war and about Scottish farming. He had a long and happy marriage with his second wife, Sally, and their two girls, Philippa and Posy.

Though the Coutts were from a long line of farmers, they all served their country during the war. Ben's eldest brother, Wally, went on to become Sir Walter Fleming Coutts, GCMG, MBE, a British colonial administrator and the Governor of Kenya in 1960. In 1961 to 1962 he was Uganda's last governor-general before independence. Brother Frank became Brigadier Frank Coutts, a policeman and soldier who had a number of prestigious appointments, including deputy lieutenant of the City of Edinburgh and president of the Scottish Rugby Union. Uncle Frank also published two books: *One Blue Bonnet*, an account of his military adventures, and a collection of reminiscences called *The Golden Thread*. The youngest brother, Philip (Uncle Phil) Coutts, spent some time in the British Foreign Service and was a district officer in Uganda with his older brother Sir Walter. He was a member of the Scottish Wool Board. Uncle Phil sadly died long before his older brothers, of a heart attack.

The mother of all these Coutts men who went on to contribute so much to their country was Rose Fleming

Coutts, a cousin of Ian Fleming, author of the James Bond books, and travel writer and adventurer Peter Fleming OBE.

Shaun's parents had divorced many years before and his mother, Criena, was a petite woman, an architect, music teacher, chef and wine connoisseur who wrote food and wine columns for the *Edinburgh Times*. Criena studied architecture at Trinity College Cambridge and was in the debating team at the same time as Philby, Burgess and Maclean were being groomed and lured into becoming Soviet spies.

Criena's family came from Ireland and her father, Sir Michael Keane, who grew up in poverty in Ireland, went on to become the Govenor of Assam in India from 1932 to 1937. He was knighted and became a popular politician. Criena Keane and her sister Kissane were presented to King George V as debutantes in London.

There were many similarities between Shaun's and my parents. Both our fathers were big men with a passion for alcohol and a love of their land and livestock. Though our mothers grew up in different worlds and in different social circumstances, they were both small women, feminists, strong willed, intellectual with passionate causes to advance the status of women. My mother has spent her lifetime fighting for the equality of Australian women. Criena, whose marriage to Ben ended as soon as the youngest son, Don, had finished school, spent many years as an active member of Amnesty International, Oxfam and lobbying the British Government for the war widow's pension as her first husband, the father of her first-born, Sarah, was killed in World War II. She married Ben Coutts after the war and they went on to have three boys, Hamish, Donald and Shaun. Hamish continues the Coutts farming name as a well-known respected Scottish farmer. Younger brother Don has recently won two Scottish BAFTAs in 2014 and 2015 for his film directing work on the children's TV series *Katie Morag* with his editor wife, Lindy Cameron.

We have had many trips to Scotland. My father-in-law Ben and I both loved writing and wrote regularly to each other. I looked forward to seeing the blue aerogramme/air letter arriving in our mail bag with his scrawling writing in his blue fountain pen. I kept all his letters and returned them to him when he was writing his books. He lived a great life and died at the age of eighty-seven in 2004.

We have maintained close contact with the family over our forty years of marriage, most recently returning in 2015 to spend time with them and in particular my stepmother-in-law, Sally Coutts, now a nimble eighty-five years of age and still judging horse events at the Highlands Show, riding her ponies and regularly walking the hills of Scotland.

On our return from our first trip to Scotland Shaun and I decided to start a family and move back to the Territory when the opportunity arose.

I missed the Territory life and wanted to go home because I knew that Mum and Bill Tapp's marriage was in disarray. Bill Tapp was drinking heavily and calling us with long phone calls in the middle of the night, drunk, crying and asking us to come home. Mum never complained but I knew that she was drinking a lot and the marriage was a mess.

I worried about my younger siblings, some of whom were at boarding school in Sydney – and Bill Tapp was not paying the school fees. The bills were piling up at Killarney; the cattle industry went into recession and the boys were removed from boarding school for a year to stay home working on the station. Shing had been going to school at Kambala in Sydney and before we went on our trip to Scotland she came to live with us to allow her to finish Year 10.

No one knew that she was pregnant when she arrived. It was a shock for all of us, including Shing. There were the unspoken thoughts of abortion and when the doctor confirmed that she was twenty-two weeks pregnant, at least that option did not have to come up. Shaun and I had not counted on having to deal with a pregnant teenager and it was decided she would go to a single mothers home in

Melbourne to have the baby. It was a difficult time for Shing, as Shaun and I both worked long hours and neither of us knew much about pregnancy, as I was barely an adult and had not been pregnant myself. We felt it would be easier for her to have the support and counselling she needed to make the decision on whether to keep the baby or not. The pressure was on young single mothers in the 1970s to adopt their babies out. After many long phone calls to the radio telephone at Killarney, Shing decided to keep her baby and return home after the birth. While Bill Tapp was not so happy about having a part-Aboriginal grandchild, Mum said that she did not want to have a grandchild who did not know where he came from.

Shing delivered the first Tapp family grandchild, a healthy baby boy named Shane, in Melbourne in June and a few days later Shaun drove down to pick them up and bring them back to Mansfield. When they didn't arrive home at the expected time, I went to work – it was the Queen's Birthday weekend and the Delatite Hotel had bumper crowds for the snow skiing season. Shaun was an excellent and responsible driver so I wasn't too worried as the time ticked by, until the boss called me to the telephone to take a call from my husband.

Shaun and Shing had been driving home into the sunset and heavy holiday traffic through Yarra Glen as two women were riding their horses along a fence line near the road. One of the horses, a stallion, spooked and bolted into the oncoming traffic. The rider fell off into the traffic, and the horse landed on the bonnet of our car, front legs thrashing through the windscreen, shattering glass onto everyone. While Shaun missed being kicked in the face by centimetres, Shing was able to lean over and cover her baby in the back seat. It was the most terrifying few minutes as the horse thrashed, the glass cutting into its legs, and people trying to pull it off the car and calm it. As luck would have it there was a veterinary surgeon in one of the cars and a farm house just 200 metres up the road. The vet helped pull the horse off the vehicle and road and tend to it, and the people in the farmhouse, who had heard the commotion and come out to inspect, were able to take Shing and the six-day-old baby to their house. Both were in shock and had little cuts on their faces from the flying glass. The family looked after them and helped get the car off the road to leave at their place. A friend of ours drove to Yarra Glen to pick up Shaun, Shing and Shane and return them home to Mansfield.

Within a year of returning from overseas, we had our first baby, Ben, delivered on a bitter cold May afternoon at the Mansfield Hospital. Ben had suffered quite a bit of trauma after getting wedged in my pelvis and, following an emergency caesarean, twelve hours after birth he was taken by ambulance to the neonatal unit in Melbourne in the middle of the night. I didn't see him again until he was seven days old.

My birthing experience was totally different to my mother's experience of having a reasonably quick labour and returning within days. Not that I had been at any of the births of my siblings; however, I had never heard of a caesarean birth. I assumed all births were natural, just like the women in the Aboriginal camp and the animals I grew up with.

It was certainly a strange experience to have to express milk with no baby on hand to drink it. However, I had a plentiful supply and it was ferried off in a stainless steel bowl into the bowels of the hospital to be used for other babies. I was in a lot of pain after the caesarean and was heavily sedated, so spent the first couple of days sleeping. Getting in and out of bed was difficult and each day I would ask how Ben was going and they would just say he was improving. Those were certainly different days for mothers and babies, who were treated much more impersonally. It is a weird feeling to be in hospital for the first time in your life, to know you have a baby out there somewhere, just trusting that he will be cared for and eventually returned to you. It was a long seven days and the anticipation about seeing my little human being was intense and scary, with all the doubts flooding in about my ability to take care of him. The day finally arrived when Ben was placed in my arms. The overwhelming love that a mother feels at this moment is a language that only mothers know. After almost three weeks in hospital Shaun and I walked out of the hospital front door with our baby boy, Ben Fleming, named after my father-in-law and my brother Ben. A big boy who has brought us so much love, heartache and endless joy over the years.

Chapter 17

BACK TO THE BUSH

WHILE I LOVED LIVING IN THE HIGH COUNTRY WITH its spectacular scenery and eccentric people, I still longed to return to the savannah plains with their burning red soil and magnificent blue skies with the horizon that goes on forever. So, in 1980, after four years in Mansfield, we left Victoria and moved back to the Northern Territory to take up a job on Victoria River Downs Station, 380 kilometres west of Katherine and Killarney's neighbouring station. VRD covers an area of 8900 square kilometres and was owned by the Hooker Corporation at the time. Shaun had taken on a position looking after the Brahman stud cattle.

Going home meant confronting my parents' messy marriage and the fact that Killarney was in deep debt. I was unprepared for the level of violence and dysfunction that had escalated over the four years we were away. Mum had continued to write big newsy letters and the odd phone call was always full of great news about the Killarney family. Never once did Mum complain to me, or to any of the family or her mother or her friends, about how badly the relationship had spiralled. She could certainly stand up for herself and often gave back as good as she received; however, there was no avoiding that Bill Tapp was a big man with two personalities, an alcoholic who was losing a grip on reality and hurting the person he loved the most in his life: my mother.

It was hard to like him at these times as he went on big drinking benders down south, squandering the hard-earned money. My brothers Billy, Sam and Joe were now managing Killarney, doing all the mustering and selling of cattle and horses, maintaining the employees and dealing with Elders without any legal ability to take control.

Mum was drinking heavily and would arrive on our doorstep bruised and battered, having driven 70 kilometres of dirt roads in the middle of the night. She would stay a few days and, as we did not have telephones, Bill Tapp would turn up at VRD to beg her to return home. On other occasions he sent one of the workers – usually Pat

Quirk, an alcoholic who would divert to get on a drunken bender for a couple of days before proceeding to VRD to cajole Mum into returning. She always went back because there were so many people to take care of.

———

Shaun, Ben and I had a great life at VRD. The station sits high on the banks of the magnificent Wickham River, which was full of barramundi and crocodiles. VRD had a population of about 150 people, which included the small outstations of Mount Sanford, Pigeon Hole and Moolooloo. These stations all operated in the far reaches of VRD because it was such a massive property and the distances were too large to take cattle back to the main station. Among the station's employees were a large camp of traditional Aboriginal people and the Aboriginal workforce, and Helimuster, a contract helicopter mustering company owned by John Weymouth that employed about fifteen people. Helimuster rented a number of the houses on the station to house their helicopter pilots and engineers.

The managers of VRD at the time were Gilbert McAntee and his wife, Gwen. The station had a store that opened twice a week, a post office, a primary school with over twenty-five students housed in large silver portable caravans, a health clinic and, most importantly, twenty-four-hour power. We lived in a long, rambling tin shed that had been upgraded with a bathroom at one end and an add-on kitchen at the other. The exterior walls were made of corrugated tin to about waist height and then fly wire to the tin ceiling; it had three internal bedrooms that had been closed in with fibro walls and tiny box windows. The bedrooms were incredibly hot and we often slept out on the verandahs, where the water sheeted in during the wet season along with millions of flying ants and stinky lavender bugs. I managed to turn the shed into a comfortable home despite the constant infestations of cockroaches, lizards, geckos and snakes.

Our house was located just 100 metres across a green-grassed area from the Big House, where the manager lived, and next to the station health clinic. The whole station gathered on rugs on the lawn in front of my house to watch Hollywood movies such as *Jaws* and *The Towering Inferno* on a huge, custom-made steel screen. The Aboriginal children loved the movies and would scream in the crucial moments, as bodies plummeted out of the burning building or the shark seemingly dived out of the screen.

We had a busy social life, gathering at the Helimuster houses and the social club for barbecues and parties. We held fundraising fetes and hosted sports days for the school, catered for weddings and engagements and made decorated cakes out of the *Australian Women's*

Weekly Children's Birthday Cookbook for our children. The women who lived with their husbands managing the outstations of Moolooloo and Mount Sanford travelled in for these functions.

Ben was a child who was forever disappearing around the station, climbing up trees and onto roofs, and once falling into an above-ground swimming pool and almost drowning when the family was away on holidays. Three days before his second birthday, I awoke in the early hours of the morning with severe stomach cramps and gushing blood that seemed to go on for hours. I was twelve weeks pregnant. I sat in the bath with cold water rinsing the blood down the drain and used towels to sleep on. The bleeding didn't seem to want to stop.

As the sun rose I finally woke Shaun to tell him what was happening and he called Sister Pat, the nurse who managed the health clinic. She determined that as I was still bleeding heavily, I would need to go to hospital in Katherine for a curette. I tried to convince her that it should all be well within a couple of hours, as I wanted to stay home and prepare for my son's party. Sister Pat would have none of it and I was evacuated out of VRD in a single-engine Helimuster plane.

I stayed in hospital for two days and arrived home in time for Ben's party, which the lovely ladies of VRD had organised while I was away.

In May 1980, the Governor-General of Australia, Sir Zelman Cowen, and his wife, Lady Anne Cowen, arrived for a visit to VRD with a large official party. A team of people had flown in a month prior to the visit to do reconnaissance and advise every one of the protocols required, such as how to address the Governor-General and Lady Cowen. As the GG was to visit the school, the teacher spent a lot of time teaching the children how to sing their song and to say 'Good afternoon, Your Excellency'. On the day, when the GG arrived in his large plane, the children, with freshly scrubbed faces, all said on cue, 'Good afternoon, Your Majesty', to which Sir Zelman graciously explained the difference.

That evening, Gilbert and Gwen McAntee hosted open-air cocktails and nibbles on the front lawn of the big house, where we all lined up to shake hands and have a little chat with the GG and his wife. They stayed overnight in the guest quarters and continued on their official trip to other parts of Australia the next morning.

It was during this time I was asked by my friends Carol Armstrong and Roylene Hill at VRD to join the newly formed Isolated Children's Parents Association (ICPA), which was a lobby group for equity and equality education in the bush, in particular for students and families who used the School of the Air and Correspondence. I met and made friends with many of the young families in the region who remain friends to this day. The Katherine ICPA held fundraising functions, dinners and fashion parades and full-scale shows that included three nights of the crazy play about a country wedding, *Dimboola*, held at Katherine Hotel Restaurant and headed by the dynamic Terry Underwood from Riveren Station. Terry held all the rehearsals over the School of the Air radios and ordered the costumes from Sydney. Shaun and I formed a lifelong friendship with Terry and John Underwood and we both performed in many of her shows over the years.

Another highlight of our social life was going home for the Killarney quarter horse sale. All the cattle stations in the area took the weekend off to attend the sale held in May each year. People would roll in on the Saturday morning in preparation for a weekend of partying and, for the more serious, to buy some horses in the sale ring under lights in the evening. My brothers and the staff of Killarney would be busy shampooing and brushing the horses' coats and polishing saddles, bridles and boots for the final presentation. Mum, of course, would be running around organising beds and meals for the auctioneer and the Elders VIPs, while Bill Tapp was busy entertaining and dealing with the buyers.

I was due to have my second child on the weekend of the Killarney horse sale in 1981. I pleaded with the doctor to not have to go to town two weeks earlier, as was the requirement, so I could go to the horse sale. He relented, as he knew it was most likely that I would go to the sale anyway. Shaun, Ben and I had a fabulous weekend at the sale as always and went to Katherine the following Monday to deliver our baby girl Megan Rose by caesarean section on 27 May.

Chapter 18

A NEW TERRITORY ADVENTURE

AS WE DROVE ACROSS THE CARPENTARIA HIGHWAY towards Borroloola on an incredibly hot day in August 1981, all our worldly goods and possessions in an old green Falcon XB with a trailer on the back, I wondered if the road was ever going to end. We were headed for McArthur River Station, 600 kilometres south-east of Katherine in the remote croc-infested river country of the Gulf, near the Queensland border, where Shaun had accepted the position as head stockman. McArthur River is a long way from anywhere, so we would not be able to get to Killarney as much as we would have liked. We had stayed at VRD for two years but there weren't a lot of avenues for promotion for Shaun, so we decided to take the opportunity to gain new experiences in one of the last frontiers of the Territory. I had no idea where we were going. Shaun had flown down for an interview after he had been told by our best friend, the Katherine vet Ross Ainsworth, that there was a job going.

As the road into the station crosses over the river and winds out into the open, you are confronted by the spectacular red escarpment of the Abner Range set against the homestead of a neat row of little white houses, white fences and sweeping lawns. Just a kilometre down the back of the station complex is the picture-postcard waterfall of Bessie Springs, which flows into the McArthur River.

McArthur River Station was owned by Colinta Holdings, the pastoral arm of Mount Isa Mines, which also owned the adjoining Tawallah and Bing Bong stations, giving them ownership of the land right through to the coast, so they could one day build a port in the Gulf of Carpentaria to export the lead silver and zinc being mined there. The place was managed by Jack and Rita Greig.

We drove down the highway on an incredibly hot day. Ben was two years old, Megan was three months old and she was strapped on the back seat in a red plastic baby bath with the safety belt around the bath to hold it in place. All our worldly goods, the total of our first five years of marriage, were piled up in the old green station wagon and a trailer.

As you drive in to the station just a few kilometres off the highway, you are greeted by a large set of white gates with the brand MRT on it. Through the gate and into the dry river bed, the road swerves up and around a great big sweeping arc out onto a black soil plain. On that plain over to the right was a pile of white buildings which turned out to be the now-closed McArthur River meatworks and a great big flat area where some new cattle yards were just being built.

Behind the cattle yards and the backdrop of the red, gold and purple rock escarpment the road took us to the actual cattle station, with lovely little white painted fences, great big lawns and massive African mahogany trees.

I was relieved that it at least looked cool and well cared for. We met Jack and Rita Greig, our new bosses. Jack was a large jovial man with a severe limp from a broken pelvis many years earlier. His hat was pushed down on his grey hair. His wife, Rita, was half his size, a tiny little lady with black hair, sparkling eyes and a reserved personality.

They took us to our new house, a cottage on stilts about a metre above ground sitting out in the middle of the green paddock. Two bedrooms, a tiny kitchen and bathroom all combined, and a laundry outside in a white tin lean-to. It wasn't long before I decorated the cottage with my trendy red-and-black '80s curtains and bedspreads, and my few souvenirs and bits of silver.

When we first arrived there were twenty-five children in the school, of which the majority were Aboriginal. There was a full-time teacher and an Aboriginal teacher's aid. The stock camp consisted of twenty Aboriginal men whose families all lived in a new camp of corrugated-iron houses built by Mount Isa Mines (MIM). The only white employees were the Greigs, the mechanic and his family, the schoolteacher, and us. There were no telephones, television or radio reception other than the Radio VJY. The Flying Doctor flew in every six weeks. The dental bus visited every second year. Boomerang Freight delivered our mail and stores fortnightly from Mount Isa. While the rest of Australia watched events unfold on TV and most homes had a video recorder, we lived blissfully in our own little world as important events were reported on the crackly radio. With snippets of news from the radio and the occasional *Australian Women's Weekly* magazine we knew that Prince Charles had married the beautiful Lady Diana Spencer, Australia had won the America's Cup, and Britain had declared war in the Falklands.

We had only been at McArthur River for about a year and Shaun was camping out with the mustering camp when I once again realised that I was having a miscarriage, and I was unable to get a message to him. Shing was visiting at the time with her son, so we decided that, rather than call the Flying Doctor – which would mean I could not take my kids – we would drive the 600 kilometres to town, me sitting on towels to sop up the bleeding. I had been ten weeks pregnant and was booked into hospital that afternoon for an overnight stay and curette.

Our first few years at McArthur were all hard work. Shaun was camping out on the station with the stock camp and I was a full-time mum to our little ones, Ben and Megan. Our social life included parties held at Bessie Springs and going into Borroloola for the annual Raft Race. We celebrated Melbourne Cup, dressing up and holding sweeps. The highlight of the year was the annual Borroloola Rodeo and going to Katherine for the Katherine Show and catching up with my family. Being so much further away limited our ability to go home to Killarney.

The pastoral company Colinta Holdings, a subsidiary of MIM, underwent expansion in Queensland and Jack and Rita Greig were promoted and transferred. That left the opportunity for Shaun to be promoted to manager and we moved into the big house in August 1984. I was thrilled to move from the two-bedroom cottage into a four-bedroom house.

Mum and I continued to write long letters to each other and she never mentioned the escalating breakdown of the marriage, though she was making plans to leave and live in Katherine.

As wife of the station manager, I was responsible for all the housing, running the men's kitchen, the guest houses and Aboriginal housing, as well as the medicine kit and all communications to the doctor, especially calling the Flying Doctor for any major injuries. Radio telephone at the big house was still the only communication until 1988, when we got real telephones and were able to put in a public phone for the staff. We managed McArthur River, Tawallah and Bing Bong stations while going through the turmoil of the brucellosis and tuberculosis eradication campaign (BTEC) that saw thousands of cattle shot out in an effort to eradicate TB from Territory cattle herds.

Our only form of sport and recreation was the local rodeos. The Borroloola Rodeo remains one of the last of the traditional bush rodeos, with an event to suit everyone. We ran the first camp-drafts in the Gulf at McArthur River in 1986 and 1987 and held horsemanship schools to increase the staff's skills and any locals who wished to attend were more than welcome.

In March 1984 the region was battered by Cyclone Kathy, with a wind intensity stronger than Cyclone Tracy, which razed the city of Darwin in 1974. Cyclone Kathy affected twenty vessels off shore, one of which sank, resulting in the death of its captain. Additionally, mangroves along the McArthur River sustained substantial damage. Once over land, Kathy rapidly weakened, losing gale-force winds within 24 hours.

It was incredible that the damage to the town of Borroloola was minimal although thousands of kilometres of bush was flattened and tidal waves affected the dugong population.

Just a year later Cyclone Sandy formed in the Gulf of Carpentaria and moved west over Bing Bong Station and Port Roper. Two fishing trawlers were beached on North Island, Bing Bong homestead was wrecked, and extensive damage was caused to vegetation and seagrass beds along the south-west Gulf coast. Surges of up to 3 metres were experienced, with turtles and pilot whales being swept ashore. The Bureau of Meteorology's Centre Island weather station recorded a maximum wind gust of 220 kilometres an hour.

Through both cyclones we sat up at night listening to the radio as the wind whipped up a frenzy around our houses. McArthur River is situated 100 kilometres west of Borroloola and we were cut off for at least a week each time as all the rivers filled up and we could not get out.

The biggest events in the region were the Borroloola Rodeo and the Brunette Downs races and both Shaun and I camp-drafted as well as barrel-raced, and entered in all the novelty events at the rodeo. I entered in the Ladies Steer

Un-decorating and the Ladies Race and Shaun hazed for me and rode pick-up at the rodeos. Our children rode and competed with us. We travelled thousands of kilometres to compete at Daly Waters, Tennant Creek, Spell Bore and Katherine. It was a major logistical exercise to get the kids, horses, trucks and ourselves to these events, but we wouldn't have missed them for anything in the world.

In 1989 I bought Fiona's Shop in Borroloola from my friend Fiona Darcy, who lived at the neighbouring Mallapunyah Springs. I changed the name to the very original name of 'Toni's Shop'. Fiona Darcy had become one of my many lifelong friends when we first moved to the Gulf. She was a woman with a good eye for business and was the founding president of our Gulf Branch of the Isolated Children's Parents' Association.

Former owner of the Shell Take Away, Dorothy McKey, came out of retirement to manage the shop for me and stayed until 1995. She was a wonderful lady who helped the Aboriginal women with their buying and budgeting. We were the only business in 'The Loo' that did not allow 'book up' – a practice that permitted people to take their purchases on a tab, not paying for the goods until their pay cheques came in. Instead, we ran a lay-by system to help the women buy the essentials and not accumulate large debts, as happened under the book-up system.

I overhauled the shop's stock, bringing in the more modern Western top boots and the Wrangler and Thomas Cook Western labels as well as a wide range of family clothing, prams, bikes, music cassettes and cassette players. We sold a comprehensive chemist line, hair-care products, camera films and scratch lottery cards. The hairdresser, known as the bush barber, came down every two months and ran a hairdressing service for the full week out of the shop, as it had a built-in hairdressing sink and mirrors. We ran Melbourne Cup fashion parades at the pub, which the young women and men loved participating in. I applied for a hawker's licence and would set up my shop on the back of a trailer at the rodeos, selling all the latest Western-wear fashion shirts and Wrangler jeans along with saddle pads and horse bandages.

When Ben was four, we lived through the terror of sitting up all night as he gasped for air in a severe asthma attack, fearing it might be the last one. The Flying Vet called in to the station that morning but was unable to take us into Katherine because his plane was not pressurised. The Air Med Doctor finally arrived in a pressurised plane and Ben and I spent a week in Katherine Hospital. In 1988, Ben was diagnosed with a rare bone disease in his hip, Perthes disease, and we travelled the 1800-kilometre round trip to Darwin countless times to visit specialists and undergo tests until finally he had an operation and spent six weeks at home in a full-body plaster.

In the bush you do what you have to do. I never had to deliver a baby but I did have to sit out on the main road just a few kilometres from the turn-off when Ronnie Raggett, a station hand, came in one morning to say there was a vehicle rollover with a dead person beside it. Shaun was away in Queensland and the stock camp was out on another big muster. I rang the police and they told me to go out and check the vehicle and wait for them. I asked Ronnie to return with me as I bundled up blankets and bandages in the hope that the person was still alive. When I arrived on the accident scene – without Ronnie, who was scared to return to sit with a dead body – I checked the man who had been thrown out of the vehicle and realised that he had been dead for a few hours. The deceased person was Frank Blakey, a stock inspector who had been in the Gulf for a number of years and had returned for a visit to his old stomping ground. He had had a few heavy days of drinking with his friends and decided to leave for Heartbreak Hotel – the Cape Crawford Roadhouse, set up by Brian Counihan in 1981 – in the early hours of the morning but had lost control of his car on a bend. I sat on the side of the road and waited for the police to arrive. No other traffic came by in that time.

One cold night in 1989, Freddy Raggett came banging on the door, asking me to go down to see his father, who was having a fit. The Raggett family had lived at McArthur River for fifty years, since the 'Old Man', Sonny Raggett, arrived there to caretake at the end of World War II. He was originally from Alice Springs and had an Afghan heritage. He told me the story of being part of the search party for Elizabeth Darcy, mother of the twelve children of the Darcy family, who went missing with her youngest son Mick in October 1944. Elizabeth and Mick did not return home after looking for donkeys. The search was officially abandoned after almost six intensive weeks, with the entry in the Police Journal reading as follows: 'Despite combined efforts ten whites and thirty Aboriginals, no trace of Mrs Darcy or son can be found. It has been suggested they caught quiet grey horse and rode away nevertheless I fear they have perished in rough hilly country south Mallapunyah where water limited. Have abandoned search.'

Sonny was in his seventies and a severe asthmatic. The camp was only 200 metres from the homestead but the old man had passed away by the time I got there. I rang the police in Borroloola and left him with his family to say goodbye. The wailing went long into the early hours of the morning as the family mourned Sonny's passing. The police arrived at about 1.00 p.m. to take his body to the mortuary. We organised to have him buried on the banks of the McArthur River just down the back and when his wife, Angelina, passed away a year later, she was buried beside him.

In 1988, my best friend, Chrissie Holt – from the neighbouring Balbirini Station – and I were spending one of our many Sunday afternoons at Bessie Springs with the kids and a couple of bottles of wine. We decided that the Gulf was sadly lacking in formal events and it was time to have an old-fashioned outback ball. That afternoon discussion was the birth of the Heartbreak Bush Ball. Sewing machines ran hot and Dianne Lane of Crazy Birds Boutique in Katherine sent us a selection of taffeta and satin evening gowns in a range of sizes and styles to try on and purchase. New clothes were ordered for the kids and old safari suits were dusted off for the men. We made trays of kabana, cheese, dips, fresh prawns and chicken wings – no easy task in the Gulf in the 1980s. Ribbons were ordered for the Matron and the Belle of the Ball, Mini Prince and Princess along with Bull of the Ball and Mickey of the Ball. We danced the night away in our ball gowns to the then popular girl band from Darwin, The Sublimes, whom we flew in for the event.

We also formed the Heartbreak Ladies Cricket Club and held fun sports days on the airstrip at Heartbreak. In 1985, a group of us formed the Cape Crawford Branch of the ICPA and a year or so later a large gathering in Borroloola formed the Gulf Branch of the Country Liberal Party. The ICPA went on to launch the inaugural Borroloola Show in 1985 and played a major role in catering at many functions in the district, including Variety Club Bashes, rodeos, the Borroloola Show and Rodeo, and the Borroloola Fishing Classic. We had barbecues and parties at Bessie Springs, cocktail parties at Fiona Darcy's at Mallapunyah Station and dinner parties at Balbirini Station.

Shaun took over as president of the Rodeo Club in the early 1990s and I had our third child, a daughter, Shannon, in October 1990. Ben and Megan attended boarding school in Darwin.

A highlight for our branch of ICPA was when Chrissie became the state president and I became the publicity officer for the Northern Territory State Council of ICPA in 1990 after a tough battle of wills at the annual general meeting in Alice Springs.

We drove the 1000 kilometres to Alice Springs with Chrissie's three children and me with baby Shannon just six weeks old. We got a flat tyre in the middle of the Barkly Tablelands, and with the possibility of not seeing a vehicle for hours, we had to change the tyre. Having had a caesarean, I could do little except stand by and watch while Chrissie and her eldest son, Daniel, twelve, tackled the changing of the heavy tyre. The spare tyre was bolted under the vehicle and when Daniel was unable to get it out, Chrissie decided she had to get under and help or we could be stuck there in the blazing November heat for hours. As we would be going straight to a reception on arrival in Alice Springs, we were dressed for the occasion. Chrissie pulled off her lovely lemon-coloured linen dress over her head and crawled under the vehicle with Daniel, in her bra, knickers and a half-slip. They eventually got the tyre changed and Chrissie wiped her hands and the red dirt off her back and put her dress back on. No one was any the wiser on our arrival in Alice Springs five hours later, as Chrissie swooped into the reception elegant and smiling as always.

We held Christmas parties at Bessie Springs for all the children in the district and Santa made a grand entrance each year either by helicopter, horse, quad bike or canoe. Despite the remoteness and isolation we still managed to celebrate Melbourne Cup with fashions of the field. The Borroloola Centenary celebrations saw us in long evening gowns, the men in dinner suits dancing the night away under the stars to the Darwin Big Band with the Chief Minister and Administrator of the NT.

By the mid-1990s there was a change in the social structure of the Gulf country from a pastoral community to a mining community. There had been a slow exodus of families from the bush and McArthur River now had a diminished population of one Aboriginal family, six white stockmen, a mechanic and bore-runner handyman and us. The school had closed. Only one of the four 'married houses' was occupied and the Aboriginal camp had been abandoned.

Mount Isa Mines decided to fire up the mine that had lain dormant for many years and work commenced on a double-lane highway to the port at Bing Bong Station in the Gulf. The Northern Territory Government extended the gas pipeline 300 kilometres from Daly Waters on the Stuart Highway to the McArthur River Mine. Once an outstation of McArthur River, Bing Bong was transformed into a shipping port to transfer the lead and zinc mined at McArthur. King Ash Bay and the Borroloola Fishing Club soon became an outer suburb of Borroloola.

Over the years we had seen a new police station, health clinic with a permanent doctor in residence, a government community centre and education centre built in Borroloola, along with the development of a whole new suburb and new housing.

We had loved every day of the thirteen years that we lived there but the time had come to take a new direction in life: to move the 500 kilometres north to Katherine, where I had bought a little dress boutique called Cool Change. Shaun didn't have a job and was a bit anxious about the move, but I was confident it wouldn't be long before he would get work. We had purchased a 25-acre block in Katherine a few years earlier so that we could take our horses with us to continue competing in show events.

By this time my mother had long left Killarney and moved to live in Katherine. She had given up drinking and was immersed in her causes, such as the establishment of the Women's Crisis Centre and actively participating in the Victoria River Branch of the Country Liberal Party.

Bill Tapp's drinking had spiralled into hell and my brothers were struggling to keep the station going whilst Bill Tapp was drinking it all deep into debt.

Chapter 19

THE BEGINNING OF THE END

IN MANY WAYS MY BROTHERS AND SISTERS AND I WERE blessed to grow up with two passionate, intelligent parents. Mum and Bill Tapp were each unique, and probably unique as a couple too – notwithstanding that occasional comparison with Elizabeth Taylor and Richard Burton. I have rarely met anyone who imbued each day with such energy as those two.

Mum's brain never stopped working (it still doesn't). She opens her eyes each day with a list of about fifty things she wants to accomplish or protest or rave about. She has never stopped thinking about all sorts of matters, from global problems to issues on Killarney that needed her attention. You hear the phrase 'force of nature' used to describe people and sometimes I think it must have been invented for Mum. She's Tropical Cyclone June, clearing everything in her path and leaving chances for a new beginning in her wake, even if it sometimes comes with a bit of destruction.

Bill Tapp had a different type of personality but he was no less a presence. He was a man of extraordinary vision, able to carry people along with him and make them believe in his vision as much as he did. Not unlike Mum, he could bruise a few people on the way, but we always had to admire his conviction in doing whatever he set his mind to. He had a very clear dream about what Killarney would become and he achieved that. Where Mum tended to think mostly about big issues, Bill Tapp would obsess about small details. When they were happy to work together, they struck an incredible balance, and I am sure that Bill Tapp could not have achieved his Killarney dream without Mum.

Over time, though, and as each turned to alcohol more and more to manage the stress in their lives, the differences between them were exacerbated and the team they had once been began to fracture, sometimes loudly. I was off living my own life with my own family when their relationship faltered and I didn't see or hear the worst of it; that was for the younger kids. Looking back, I realise how lucky

I was to have lived with Bill Tapp in his prime – to have seen the man of vision at work. I didn't really have to deal with him when his alcoholism grew worse, I just had to deal with how it affected Mum, because she would show up at my door needing to escape.

Mum made innumerable attempts to leave Bill Tapp. Their bond had always been a strong one, though, so it took time to be stretched out of shape. I can't say it was ever broken, because there were the ten of us kids, for one thing, and Killarney was as much a part of Mum as of Bill Tapp, and she could never stay away for long.

It wasn't until 1985 that Mum made a definitive break, buying a house in Katherine. She would later say that even though she and Bill Tapp had been fighting for years, she still didn't really comprehend what was going on. She didn't realise that Bill Tapp's behaviour was caused by his being an alcoholic; she thought he could stop drinking anytime but he didn't want to. She didn't realise that he couldn't stop drinking by this stage, that it was a physical addiction he had no way of controlling.

After Mum left him, Bill Tapp made attempts to get off the grog – he would last a couple of months then break out. Finally, though, the alcohol took over everything. Bill Tapp would run away to Darwin and Sydney; according to Mum, he got mixed up with prostitutes and heroin addicts. He would stay in expensive hotels, stocking up on grog and locking out the world so he could get drunk. It would never have suited Bill Tapp to go on an alcoholic bender in a rundown motel – he always wanted the best, so he'd spend tens of thousands of dollars at a time in the Hilton in Sydney, for example. The amount of money he spent in total on what can only be described as extreme self-destructive behaviour would amount to millions of dollars.

Mum's divorce from Bill Tapp was long and acrimonious and despite Mum successfully putting a caveat on Killarney to stop Bill Tapp spending money on unnecessary items until the property settlement was finalised in the Supreme Court of the Northern Territory, Bill Tapp went on long, expensive holidays to Sydney in attempts to find new funds to finance Killarney. In one of his crazier schemes he managed to secure a loan to develop a gutta-percha plantation, some airy-fairy tree-growing project on Roper Valley that someone had convinced him would bring in a good income. He wanted to pay off debts to pimps and other 'hazy underworld characters', as my mother called them. The loan was successful, the project never went ahead and the money was all spent on other things.

As my brothers grew up and left school, they returned home to look after the stations, Joe and William remaining at Killarney while Billy managed the new property of Maryfield Station, south-east of Killarney. Bill Tapp's drinking and long disappearances down south were now an accepted part of life, even though he went in and out of hospital in attempts to dry out. Once, he ended up on drink-driving charges. The family was threatened by pimps, heroin addicts and prostitutes. There were, Mum said, two women who lived in Darwin who got thousands and thousands of dollars from him.

There were plenty of other stresses on Bill Tapp, too. The Territory cattle industry was almost closed down when the Northern Territory Government introduced the brucellosis and tuberculosis eradication program (BTEC) to clean out the diseases from Territory cattle herds in the mid-1980s. This involved the government conducting mass shootings of hundreds of thousands of head of livestock across the Territory, and not being able to fairly compensate the pastoralists for the losses, which almost brought the industry to its knees. The properties ended up worth very little as the owners could not afford to restock with new cattle. Before the BTEC, Killarney had between 28 000 and 35 000 head of cattle. There was a big destock in 1989 and they sold 10 000 head to reduce the debt. There were about 5000 head of cattle shot out and about 12 000 head destocked following the BTEC program, so that was almost half the herd cut over a fairly short period of time. Killarney was left with a herd of around 18 000.

It wasn't just the financial aspect of this that worried Bill Tapp, a man who obsessed over the welfare of the smallest creature. The destocking process was hardly kind to cattle. The animals were shot by the government stock inspectors from a helicopter out in the paddocks, leaving carcasses strewn across Killarney.

The cattle were hunted from the air, with no concern for their welfare, since they were about to be shot anyway. My brother Ben and some of the others who had to deal with it tried to reason with the government men, saying that they wanted to carry out the program their own way, at a time they set – the way they'd always handled cattle. But they weren't allowed; they had to get those cattle destroyed at the pace the government wanted.

Bill Tapp had trouble handling this, of course; he was a man who liked to think things through and do them properly. The shoot-outs distressed him greatly, and Ben and I are not the only members of our family who believe that this program contributed to Bill Tapp's turning further into the blind relief that alcohol gave him. Soon, it wasn't just alcohol, he also became addicted to the prescription medications Valium and Mogadon.

Even though Mum was divorced from Bill Tapp, she was still keeping an eye on him. She has since regretted that she didn't understand more about Bill Tapp's addictions. She thinks she would have done something about it, because certainly she believed that his doctors weren't: Bill Tapp was given prescriptions for those drugs whenever he wanted them. Maybe the doctors thought they were helping him, but they would only have had to look at Bill Tapp to realise that he wasn't well. He aged dramatically over this time, became puffy with the drink, a far cry from the handsome man who had won my mother's heart. In the defence of everyone involved, it was an era when addictions simply weren't discussed. As long as alcoholics kept functioning, no one asked any questions. We'd had so many of them working on Killarney and none of us asked any questions there, either. And drug addictions were often invisible – if you had a prescription from your doctor, only you and the chemist knew what was going on. It was impossible to help someone who didn't want to be helped. I guess it still is. And I don't think Bill Tapp wanted to be helped. He had pride, and he still had his dream – all the financial problems, added to the loss of so many of his cattle, would have seemed like the destruction of that dream. He wouldn't have thought to stop and contemplate everything he'd done up to that point. All his achievements on Killarney – including raising a family of ten – wouldn't have counted for anything. He hadn't been able to sustain it. He hadn't been able to fulfil that ideal he'd formed long ago: cattle king.

The people around him didn't help. I don't mean Mum or my brothers, who were also affected by what was happening on the stations. I mean the people who had an idea of the bigger financial picture – the ones who were processing the accounts. No one would stand up to him, and he'd long stopped paying attention to Mum. Mum, meanwhile, would ring around, telling these people of her concerns about Bill Tapp's spending and drinking.

'Oh yeah, June, we know old Bill,' they'd say. 'We're just waiting for something to happen.'

We would never find out why they wanted Bill Tapp's life to collapse – why they were so keen to see him fall. We had our theories. At the time, it just seemed like extreme callousness, and it made us desperately sad. We had tried to stop him and we couldn't. We had pleaded with the people who gave him loans to stop giving him money and they wouldn't. If Bill Tapp was his own worst enemy, he certainly had some helpers along the way.

After Bill Tapp had done something diabolical, he would always apologise for his behaviour. It didn't stop him doing more terrible things, though. Once he went off to buy a new ute and came back with three Mercedes-Benz. That sort of thing became typical of a man who had once seemed so in control of himself. We didn't know what was wrong with him then but we've worked it out since: he had bipolar disorder, and he self-medicated, whether it was by buying things or drinking. He'd say, 'I've bought a car so everyone can have a nice car', or he'd buy new

TV systems, then he'd feel enormous guilt and have big arguments with everybody. There was a constant cycle of guilt and recrimination.

It's amazing that he managed to hold things together for as long as he did without someone doing something to stop him. But that was due to the isolation of the place – he wasn't accountable to the outside world. It wasn't the same as living in a house in town where there are lots of people around you and an expected standard of behaviour. On Killarney he was like the premier of a state – he was the kingpin; he could do what he wanted.

In 1987 Bill Tapp caused problems amongst the boys by giving William power of attorney. Ben didn't like that, and Joe didn't like it either, because for a start William was the younger brother. The whole episode drove a big wedge between Ben, Joe and William. Ben believed that Bill Tapp gave the power of attorney to William because he was younger and Bill Tapp had a lot more sway with William than with Joe or Ben. He also did it, Ben believed, to satisfy Elders, because they had been putting the pressure on Bill Tapp to give the authority to someone else so they could deal with that new person when Bill Tapp took off and got on the grog. Joe and Ben were more likely to stand up to Bill Tapp than the teenage William would, and they were constantly arguing with Bill Tapp about buying and selling cattle. Joe and Ben were just trying to save the place – to save Killarney. Bill Tapp couldn't see that.

At the end of 1987, Ben moved down south to Brisbane with the intention of leaving the Territory altogether. He'd had a couple of big blues with Bill Tapp about the money that Bill Tapp was spending hand over fist – what little BTEC compensation money there was had been taken by Bill Tapp for his personal expenditure, and not used to reduce the debt to Elders; Bill Tapp wouldn't even contemplate a debt-reduction plan. Ben was also angry that Bill Tapp wasn't trying to get Elders under control because he hated it when those Elders fellas 'came out and acted like they owned the place'.

'You felt like you were working for them,' Ben said. 'I wanted to get rid of them.'

My brothers could see that there was a way out of the debt and that it could be brought under control reasonably easily, but Bill Tapp wasn't listening, whether because he thought he knew best or because he just didn't want to know about the problems.

After Ben moved to Queensland William and Bill Tapp rang him in February 1988 with the idea of buying Roper Valley Station. Ben had been contract mustering and bull catching on Roper Valley so he knew what the place was like. William and Bill Tapp told him that he could do what he wanted there. Despite the temptation, though, Ben said that he didn't think they should be buying anything then – instead, he thought they should be selling to get out of debt. Ben was torn: he wanted to go – he liked the place, and he knew he could make a go of it because there was a lot of bush cattle there. He also knew that it would never work. So he said no. By this stage the decision had been made on Mum and Bill Tapp's property settlement and a substantial amount of money also had to be paid to her.

However, while Ben was in Katherine to pick up his gear, Bill Tapp had arranged an inspection of Roper Valley. Ben went with Bill Tapp to the bank and made it known that he didn't think that buying the place was a good idea. Bill Tapp's solution to that was to not take Ben with him the next time. Westpac refused Bill Tapp and the Commonwealth Bank knocked him back too, but in the end Elders gave Bill Tapp the $1.2 million he needed to buy Roper Valley, which he did in April 1988. Ben moved there not long after to run the place.

From that day, though, the writing was on the wall. The debt on Killarney was about $2.5 million, including what was owed on Maryfield, and then Bill Tapp had another $2.5 million of debt with the payout to Mum and the purchase of Roper Valley. The interest rates were at

18 per cent and, on some of the debt, up to 25 per cent, so that $5 million debt rapidly grew.

But Bill Tapp didn't stop there – he went on to buy Western Creek Station in 1989. He also bought more cars, cattle, a road-train, helicopters and state-of-the-art televisions and phone systems, all funded by Elders GM. Every single purchase Bill Tapp or the station made, whether it was fruit and vegetables for the workers or a new property, had to be invoiced to Elders. They ran his day-to-day accounts and approved everything down to the horseshoe nails.

Elders kept lending him money even though they were acutely aware of his increasing debt and inability to pay, and despite my brothers pleading with them to not allow Bill Tapp to spend any more money. Bill Tapp was the sole owner of Killarney and as such there was no recourse against him, no way to stop him from financially ruining himself. There were no shareholders or board of directors to remove him. Bill Tapp made all the decisions and Elders weren't prepared to stop him either. Despite the debt, normal trading continued. Killarney sold 10 000 head of cattle at an average of $450 a head, which was an income of $4.5 million alone. So the boys believed that if this money was put back into paying the debt they should have been in a reasonable financial state and certainly nowhere near receivership or bankruptcy. When Bill Tapp went to Elders for the money for the property settlement payout and Roper, the projected budget for that year did not include the sale of the 10 000 head. The budget was for a normal trading year. It was a mistake that set the scene for what was to come.

Chapter 20

FULL CIRCLE

THROUGHOUT HISTORY, EMPIRES HAVE COLLAPSED. IN retrospect, the signs were always there – we can read our ancient history and nod knowingly, sure that if only we'd been around when the Ancient Greek and Roman and Egyptian civilisations crumbled, we could have told them how to stop the inexorable process. The Greeks probably had it right when they talked about hubris being such a danger to people and societies, even if they didn't recognise it in themselves. No one's learnt anything from those ancient lessons, though, and when you live inside a collapsing empire, you don't always see the walls coming down until it's far too late. You see the cracks – just as we saw the cracks in Bill Tapp – but you don't realise that those cracks connect. From wall to wall, they join up, until one day the whole thing splits and you're left sitting in rubble, hoping that the dust will settle eventually.

After years of extending Bill Tapp a line of credit that ran into the millions, in 1990, Elders GM, now Elders IXL, moved in to take over the properties that they had financed him to buy. They wanted to put those properties into receivership and administration. It was a clear sign that those cracks in the city walls were joining up. Still, Bill Tapp did nothing to repair them – because he was deeply incapable of it by then. It would be an understatement to say that he was out of control.

At the end of 1991, Bill Tapp agreed to sign authority of the properties to Billy, Joe, Ben, William and Daniel and Elders so they could address the debt, hopefully retain some of the pastoral business and start their lives over again. Sam was living in New Zealand and the four girls were not included in any of the considerations. Before Bill Tapp signed, he and the boys had a meeting with Elders in October 1990 in Katherine to discuss what they could do to trade out of the debt. They floated the idea that they would put all three places on the market and, if not, that they would sell as many cattle as possible.

It was agreed that all the properties, Killarney, Maryfield and Mountain Valley stations, would be advertised for sale to clear the now $11.1 million debt. When Elders went away, they had a piece of paper that was all signed, except the stamp duty of about $500 000 had to be paid before it would become a legal document of transfer to the boys. So my brothers thought everything was well on the way to being settled – that they'd be set up with a debt-reduction budget and they could trade their way out of debt. What they didn't realise was that the stamp duty was not paid.

The sale tenders were put out by Elders GM/IXL/ Fosters Brewing in early December 1991 and closed on 17 December 1991. Only allowing two weeks of advertising to sell over $30 million worth of remote Northern Territory cattle properties seemed to display an arrogance and lack of concern by the company for the man they had courted like royalty for over twenty years. The pastoral industry was still recovering from the BTEC campaign: cattle numbers were low and cattle properties were not saleable. It might have seemed to the casual observer that they hadn't really wanted to make much money on the properties.

By January 1992, Bill Tapp's health had deteriorated dramatically. My brothers had already rescued him from drinking binges in Darwin, Sydney and Brisbane, and put him into hospital. He would undergo a detox and leave overnight, regularly paying a taxi to take him from Katherine out to Killarney to get home or from Killarney to Katherine to get a flight to Brisbane or Sydney. Or he'd drive himself to the airport – he'd lost his driver's licence but continued to drive when it suited him. Mum returned to Killarney sporadically to clean the large family house where Bill Tapp now lived alone. Mum would try to nurse him back to some form of reasonable health by ensuring that he ate, showered and cut back on alcohol. Despite being a big man, he was suffering from malnutrition due to the heavy drinking and a bad diet.

On 7 January 1992, Bill Tapp, Joe and William were asked to go to Katherine for another meeting with Elders, at the Paraway Motel. Everyone thought they were going to discuss a plan to pay back the debt to Elders with a ten-year financial management plan.

My mother had returned to Killarney to take care of Bill Tapp and was standing alone on the front verandah of the big house as the receiver-appointed managers arrived. Mum hadn't heard from Bill Tapp and the boys about what was happening in Katherine; she didn't know that Elders had already appointed a receiver and had sent people out on the road to all the properties at the same time to take over the stations before the meeting in Katherine had even begun. She offered them a cup of tea and wasn't really taking notice of what was being said – until the penny dropped. They were putting Killarney into receivership.

A couple of Toyotas and an aeroplane arrived carrying more men. Suddenly there were people all over the place.

'They just walked straight into the doors of the men's quarters as if they owned the place,' Mum said. They had arrived to take over Killarney, putting notices on all the doors – the office, the men's quarters, the kitchen. They all looked very official.

Mum wasn't too sure what was happening and rang the boys in Katherine to tell them that all these people had turned up.

A few hours later, Joe and William returned home without Bill Tapp. They knew they'd been deceived by the Elders people they had trusted to help them trade out of debt. It was heartbreaking to see long-time friends of my brothers turn up as appointed managers to take over the stations. They had clearly been cultivated by Elders in the months leading up to the receivership. No one could shake the very unsettling idea that the scheme had been underway for quite a while, as Bill Tapp and the boys had unknowingly gone about their business at Killarney.

Mum and the boys sat with the receiver and Elders on the front verandah. The interlopers tried to talk them into taking $5000 each and relocating. Five thousand dollars to walk away from their heritage and their father's dream.

They kept the conversation going but, Mum said, they knew they didn't have to accept the money.

While they were all sitting around the telephone rang; William went to answer it.

'Who was that?' he was asked when he returned.

'It's President Bush,' he replied, 'and he said to tell everyone to leave the place.'

The caller was, of course, Bill Tapp, who by then had flown to Brisbane with some Elders money.

Mum stayed at Killarney that night, although she had a fitful sleep. In the middle of the night she got up to mop the floor, an old therapy for her when she was worrying about something.

As the first rays of daylight rose over Killarney, William came into the house and declared that he wasn't going to tolerate what was going on. He wasn't going to bow to Elders; he wasn't going to be hunted off Killarney. Mum's memory is that she threw the mop in the corner and said, 'Yeah, stuff 'em! If it's a fight they want, it's a fight they get.' That sounds like something she'd say – and something she'd do. Sure enough, the fight was on.

Mum rang her brother Jimmy Forscutt to ask him who she could contact to get some advice. He told Mum to ring Dennis Collins, a former politician in Alice Springs, and Dennis Collins gave her the name of a man in Victoria: Dennis O'Hair. Dennis was a solicitor who had represented a number of families who had been dealt the same hand by big companies that had tried to push families off their farms. He was told about Elders turning up and putting their official-looking pieces of white paper on all the doors. He knew that it was likely that Elders had not done their background work properly because they didn't want us to know what was going on. There was an official procedure for such things but Elders hadn't followed it. The pieces of paper were a bluff.

Dennis said to William, 'Go and tell them to get off your place. You do it straightaway and tell each one individually.'

Mum and William drove to where they knew the Elders men were gathered.

'I want you all to be gone in twenty minutes,' said William.

It worked: they left. They had underestimated the Tapp family and their ability to fight for their rights. They knew they didn't have any right to come on to Killarney and try to force the family off. They'd been relying on the fact that we might not know our rights in the situation – that we wouldn't realise that their 'notices' were worthless. They knew they'd been caught out, though, and that is why they left immediately. Where luck had been on our side was that we were a big family and had a lot of support. We had connections – people who could help us or tell us who to call for help. One could imagine the pressure there would be on an individual person facing up to this type of thing with a company that big. Still, everything was snowballing and we were all trying to do our bit to salvage the situation. Despite the circumstances, everyone had been pretty civilised.

So we had won that first battle with Elders, but the war was still ahead. There was always going to be far more at stake for the Tapps than for Elders. Elders wanted their money, and so they wanted the land that could bring the money to them. But Killarney was our home. It was Bill Tapp's creation, and his ruin, and we were prepared to fight for it.

The family fought to get a fair receiver appointed and the Northern Territory Supreme Court Judge, David Angel, appointed Mr Frank Johnston of KPMG Peat Marwick Darwin in March 1992.

Legal skirmishes and court appearances occurred on a weekly basis as the family fought to stay on the properties. They employed Michael Maurice QC and Darwin law firm Phillip and Mitaros to fight the case while Elders headed up a legal team of over twenty people. The good working relationship established with the first court-appointed receiver, Frank Johnston, came to a tragic end following his death in a car rollover on the way to a meeting in Katherine.

The court appointed a new receiver, Bob Cowling, who attempted to immediately evict the families from the stations. The court ruled in favour of the family and they remained on the stations, but were unable to participate in or carry out any work. Ben finally left Roper Valley and Billy left Maryfield to live in Katherine as it became untenable for them to live just metres away from the people forcing them off their properties.

The rats came out of the woodwork, all trying to get their piece of Killarney. Former long-time family friends tendered for mustering and management contracts and were appointed by the receiver. They moved into the Tapp family homes that had been built on virgin outback country by Mum and Bill Tapp thirty years earlier.

The small victory against Elders was not enough to save Bill Tapp. Over the years he had been in and out of hospital and rehab in an attempt to control his drinking, but there's only so many times a human body can go through that before it gives up.

In the final days of Bill Tapp's life, Mum continued to return to Killarney periodically to look after him; she bathed him and cleaned the big old house in which he now lived alone – that once was home to all twelve of us.

After one final admission to the Katherine Hospital in May 1992, Bill Tapp discharged himself on 21 May and paid over $300 for a taxi to take him back to Killarney. The next day my youngest brother, Daniel, who still lived at Killarney, seeing how sick his father still was, convinced Bill Tapp to return to Katherine Hospital. Daniel told him he would pick him up the next morning and take him back to Katherine Hospital to make sure he went.

When Daniel arrived, he found his father dead in the wood-framed king-size bed that had been built for him and Mum when they first built the house in the late 1960s. It was a lonely, inevitable death for a man who had lived and loved hard.

When Bill Tapp died, Shaun and I were living at McArthur River Station, 580 kilometres south-west of Katherine, with our three children. I owned a variety store in Borroloola for a number of years and drove the 200-kilometre round trip every week to do the ordering and catch up with my manager, Dorothy McKey.

On the morning of 23 May 1992, I arrived at the shop to be met by a request to urgently ring my mother in Katherine. My mother never said 'urgent' unless it really was. When I rang, Mum told me that Bill Tapp had died overnight at Killarney. It was my son Ben's birthday. For a moment I felt the paradox of what was happening but I couldn't dwell on it. This was life, in all its cycles, turning. News of Bill Tapp's death was not a surprise; however, nothing prepares you to hear those words. While I felt very sad, I also felt a little relief for Bill Tapp and for my brothers and the people living and working at Killarney.

Bill Tapp was buried at Killarney on 3 June, the day after what would have been his sixty-third birthday. We had all seen Bill Tapp's end coming and had tried to help him. No one will ever know what was in Bill Tapp's mind that prevented him from accepting how much we all wanted him to stay around. In his last years, he seemed determined to destroy himself; in the process, he destroyed everything he'd ever worked for.

The one thing he did not destroy was his family. He had tested us – Mum in particular – but we were still intact. His ten children were all alive and healthy. We had our differences from time to time but we still worked as a family. Perhaps, after everything he had achieved with Killarney, his family is the true testament to the majesty of Bill Tapp.

Chapter 21

THE SUN SETS ON KILLARNEY

THE FAMILY FOUGHT THE ELDERS TAKEOVER IN THE Supreme Court of the Northern Territory for over two years, citing that Elders GM ignored its fiduciary duty when dealing with Bill Tapp, making financial deals and lending him large amounts of money when they knew that he was an alcoholic and was incapable of making the right decisions.

A paper trail emerged showing that Elders had planned the events of January 1992 well beforehand – before the meeting at the end of 1991, in fact, when the boys and Bill Tapp thought they'd worked out a plan to trade through the debt. Elders had written to people and had appointed receivers prior to the meeting in Katherine in January 1992.

None of us ever had any idea that these decisions were being made about the property that we held so dear. The worst thing was that Bill Tapp and the boys knew a lot of the people contacted by Elders and they had never said anything or given an inkling of what was going on. We were totally unprepared because the Elders people who had been considered friends and colleagues never let on that they knew what was happening. Betrayal seems too mild a word for what we felt when it all came to light.

Despite having the best legal representation headed by one of Australia's best Queen's Counsels, Michael Maurice, in court, and a good case to argue, there was only a finite amount of money that the family could afford to spend fighting a multinational company the size of Elders; we decided to make an out-of-court settlement to allow everyone to get on with their lives and have some money to start again.

After so many decades, we had lost Killarney, the family home, and Maryfield with an out-of-court settlement to retain Roper Valley Station and a financial payout. We were to continue to fight a Supreme Court battle in another case against the Northern Territory government seeking compensation for the thousands of head of cattle from the BTEC shoot-out. This case had commenced while Bill

Tapp was still alive and was finally settled out of court about two years after his death. The case set a precedent for cattlemen but it would prove to be the only successful challenge to the Territory Government.

My mother was the rock who got everyone through the court cases and the family feuds about Bill Tapp's behaviour. Her meticulous and obsessive diary-keeping documented the meetings and conversations with Elders GM and government officials and the dates of Bill Tapp's stays in hospital and rehab throughout the years. Mum had kept every paper clipping and letter about every meeting ever held between Elders, lawyers, government officials and my brothers, Billy, Ben, Sam, Joe, William and Daniel, who were trying to save the family home.

As the dust settled on family feuding and the court case, four of my brothers – Joe, Ben, William and Daniel – took on the ownership of Roper Valley Station. Billy did a deal with our mother and took over Western Creek Station on the Sturt Plateau, 250 kilometres south of Katherine. Sam, Shing, Kate and I took a financial settlement according to the will. Caroline contested the appointment of Ben as the executor of the will, deciding who should lead the court cases and control the money. She also contested the expenditure on the case and her entitlement in the will. She received a further settlement.

Just a short time after the boys settled at Roper Valley Station, a land claim was made by the traditional owners for the Roper Valley homestead area, which has great cultural significance to the people of the region. They reclaimed the homestead, cattle yards and 100 square kilometres, and paid a nominal amount of compensation to the boys. My brothers had lost their home for the second time within five years and had to start again, this time subdividing the remaining country into separate properties of about 800 square kilometres each. They had to relocate the cattle and build new paddocks and yards, establish water supply and build new homes just as Bill Tapp had done all those years ago as a young man at Killarney with a big dream.

EPILOGUE

ON 19 DECEMBER 2015, MY MOTHER AND SEVEN OF US, with our families, drove the 270 kilometres to Killarney, to put a plaque on Bill Tapp's grave, twenty-three years after his death. The plaque reads, 'Killarney stands as a monument to his vision and contribution to the Northern Territory horse and cattle industry'.

It was not a sad occasion, just a walk down memory lane, a time of reflection about Bill Tapp's life, pride in his contribution to the development of the Northern Territory pastoral industry and a celebration of our family and its strength and resilience. Bill Tapp is buried just a few hundred metres from our old home, between two large fig trees and close to the water trough where the stud bull Oregon and stallion Commando would come in to water each day when Bill Tapp was the King of Killarney, and where the pink galahs boisterously line the edge of the trough each afternoon as the red sun sets in the west.

Killarney has changed little. The big house still has its large rooms and sweeping lawns, and the arched gateway covered in the purple bougainvillea that I walked through on Bill Tapp's arm on my wedding day all those years ago. The school no longer has the laughter of all those little kids trying to escape as soon as they could. It is now a house for employees. The recreation area is now all closed in with a big television on the wall, the men's quarters have verandahs, the chook house is now a carport and there is a large machinery shed. The store and the men's kitchen remain the same, as does the old wood barbecue near the first tree Mum ever planted on Killarney. The cattle yards remain a dominant feature, as do the large flame-red poinciana trees and the neat rows of houses.

On 12 December 2015, my mother June celebrated her eightieth birthday. She gave up drinking and smoking soon after leaving Killarney and has never taken either up again. She retains her enthusiasm for championing causes, currently the 'Don't Frack the Territory' campaign, headed by Daniel, who is the only brother to have retained his original property on the Roper River. She has twenty-four grandchildren and twelve great-grandchildren. She still reads all the newspapers, keeps detailed daily journals and writes weekly letters to the editor.

Sam lives on his rural property in Katherine. Joe, Ben and William sold their properties and have moved to Queensland and New South Wales, where they all thrive and excel in breeding cattle and training top-class camp-drafting and cutting horses. Billy has been employed in the mining industry in the Northern Territory for the past decade. Caroline continues to live in Darwin and Kate is an artist and high school teacher in Sydney. Shing suffered a stroke in 1999 and, following a marriage break-up, remarried and lives with her husband on her rural property in Katherine.

I continue to live in Katherine with my husband, Shaun, and our children, Ben and his wife Darcy and their girls Cassey and Chelsea, and our daughters, Megan and Shannon. I have been an elected member of Katherine Town Council for over ten years and have had a variety of life changes, including battling breast cancer in 2013. I now work for a regional council that services 5000 people and covers an area of 150 000 square kilometres. It includes Killarney.

We all did all right in the end. We have all survived and led good, fruitful lives and I am sure this is a result of the way Mum and Bill Tapp brought us up: there were few allowances made for us being children; we were expected to know right from wrong, to do our jobs on the station and help each other out. We pulled together as a family even in the toughest of times, through the court case, and we grew as individuals.

I don't miss Killarney now because it is always in me. Red dirt, the heat, the magnificent dry seasons, the lush rains of the wet season; the songs of Slim Dusty or of Old Dora and Old Daisy; Micko's cakes, sugar-bag and johnny-cakes; the imaginary footprint of a debil debil. The swaying movement of thousands of cattle streaming down the fence line towards the cattle yards, the smell of the dust and the branding iron, and of rib bones cooking on coals. All these things will never leave me.

My brothers and sisters tearing around the homestead, my mother's wild intelligence and flashing eyes, Bill Tapp's dark, penetrating gaze and his mighty dream fill my heart with love and appreciation.

Killarney shaped who I am – who we all are, including Mum. Even though I am happy to live in town now, I would change nothing about the years I spent growing up on the station. My sunburnt childhood was full of love, fun, danger and adventures, as every kid's life should be.

Killarney made me tough when I needed to be, and it taught me how to take care of people.

Just as the Aboriginal people have a deep connection to the land and the songlines, I feel that same spiritual connection to Killarney. My family and all those crazy characters are part of me. Forever.

ACKNOWLEDGEMENTS

MANY OF THE PEOPLE THAT I HAD THE PRIVILEGE TO grow up with in those early innocent days have lived tragic lives ending in suicide, murder, domestic violence and debilitating diseases such as cancer, alcoholism and diabetes. Others were able to return to their country and happily live out their final days with their families and culture. I hope that I have been able to honour them in all their crazy ways, by sharing these stories of a very special time.

Thank you to my publisher Sophie Hamley for believing in me and in the story. Thank you to the Hachette Australia team for making my dream come true.

Thank you to my dear friends in our local writing group, the Katherine Region of Writers (KROW), who have always encouraged me to keep writing and telling the Killarney story.

Thank you also to the NT Writers Centre, who have provided great support to me and to Territory writers, and to Varuna, The National Writers House in the Blue Mountains for the opportunity to work on my book in that beautiful house.

My mother, my husband and children, the Tapp family and this Territory I live in, are my rock and my inspiration.

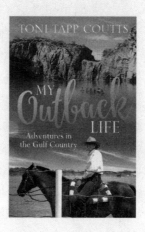

The sequel to the bestselling *A Sunburnt Childhood*

Having grown up on the massive Killarney cattle station near Katherine, NT, Toni Tapp Coutts was well prepared when her husband, Shaun, took a job at McArthur River Station in the Gulf Country, 600 kilometres away near the Queensland border.

Toni became cook, counsellor, housekeeper and nurse to the host of people who lived on McArthur River. She made firm friends, created the Heartbreak Ball and started riding campdraft in rodeos all over the Territory.

In the midst of this busy life she raised three children and saw them through challenges; she kept in touch with her large, sprawling Tapp family, and she fell deeply in love with the Gulf Country.

Filled with the warmth and humour readers will remember from *A Sunburnt Childhood*, this next chapter in Toni's life is both an adventure and a heartwarming memoir, and will introduce readers to a part of Australia few have experienced.